Complete Guide to Internet Privacy, Anonymity & Security

Matthew Bailey

www.cogipas.com

A Nerel Publication

A Nerel Publication (www.nerel-online.com).

ISBN-13: 978-3-9503093-0-0

ISBN-10: 3-9503093-0-6

Version 1.1 (A11)

Contents at a Glance

Table of Contents

Chapter 1: Introduction

Why You Need this Book

There is no question that the Internet provides many benefits, but it also poses a range of privacy and security risks.

This book is about how to protect yourself from those privacy and security risks. You will learn how to protect your communications and personal information from a range of people who may have malicious intent and who could not care less about trampling on your privacy or personal security for their own benefit. The people you have to protect yourself from may include professional identity thieves to casual snoops to determined hackers to rogue elements.

This book, the Complete Guide to Internet Privacy, Anonymity and Security (or "COGIPAS" for short), along with the companion website www.cogipas.com, contains all the unbiased and independent information and recommended services and software that you will ever need to protect your privacy and security.

About this Book and How to Use it

This book tries to achieve the delicate balance between explaining what you need to know and how it all works. In the end, this is a manual that must be accessible to both casual and advanced computer users alike. This is not always an easy task.

Each part and chapter in this book starts with the most fundamental concepts and then gets more and more advanced as it unfolds. If you are a beginner, you may wish to stop at each chapter once the material starts getting too advanced. As your interest in these topics grows you can always revisit the materials and expand your knowledge.

More advanced users may wish to do just the reverse: flip through the start of each part or chapter as a refresher and then pay closer attention to the materials that are new or less familiar.

How this Book is Organized

The contents of this book are divided into four main parts:

> **Part I** covers **The Basics** and includes chapters on Risks at a Glance; Importance of Good Passwords and Passphrases; Avoiding Identity Theft; Social Networking Sites and Online Forums; Protecting Yourself from Malware; Basic Windows Security; Using Firewall Software; Dangers of Wireless Networks and "Hotspots".

> **Part II** outlines **Safeguarding your Computer and Being Safe Online** and includes chapters on Covering Your Tracks and Washing Up; Protecting Your Identity and IP

Address with Anonymous Surfing; Getting Downloads Using Torrents and Peer-to-Peer (P2P); Encrypting Your Files to Keep them Safe; Wiping Your Sensitive Data; Using Email, Webmail and Remailers; Usenet Newsgroups; and Chat, IRC and Instant Messaging.

Part III covers **Special Interests** and includes chapters on Are They Up to No Good?; Workplace and Small Office or Home Office (SOHO); Keeping Your Children Safe; and Shopping Safely Online.

This book also includes **COGIPAS 'Top Tips' for Internet Privacy, Anonymity and Security** as well as a comprehensive **Glossary** and **Index**.

About the Sister Website

The website www.cogipas.com complements this book with up-to-date materials, news and links to video tutorials, as well as links to the COGIPAS Facebook presence.

The page www.cogipas.com/links/ collects in one place all of this book's links for easy navigating and to save you from having to type website addresses into your browser. Please note that some website addresses appearing in this book begin with http*s* (don't forget to type in the 's').

In particular, should recommendations that are presented in this book change, this will be reflected as much as possible through updates on www.cogipas.com.

About the Symbols Used in this Book

To highlight or expand on certain points in a chapter, various text boxes are used.

    ! Warning ! -   related warnings, dangers or risks to be aware of

    More About -   facts, figures or technical explanations often for advanced users

    Top Tip -   hidden gems and other tips and tricks

When this book explains menu choices, either for using software or for navigating a website, the selections will be separated by the symbol '>'. For example, to print a document in most word processing software you would select the following menu choices, *File* > *Print*, which means you first choose the "File" menu item and then select the "Print" option in that menu.

When this book suggests search terms, either in an Internet search engine or for software on your computer, the search string will be surrounded by "double quotes". When entering the suggested search string in the search engine or software, you should *omit* the quotes.

About the Screenshots Used in this Book

You may notice that some screenshots will have parts **blurred** or **smudged out**. This has been done to remove any identifying information, including trademarks and personal data, which are not necessary to illustrate the techniques shown in the screenshots.

Please also note that screenshots in this book reflect the most recent versions of software at the time of publishing, including Windows 7 and Internet Explorer 9. Of course, as software is updated and changed, your screens may vary somewhat from the screenshots presented here. Check the www.cogipas.com website for updates.

About Copyright and Downloads

This book assumes that you are using the Internet and all its various tools, including the web, email, Usenet and peer-to-peer (P2P), for legitimate, non-copyright infringing uses. You should obtain and share your downloads responsibly and legally.

PART I - THE BASICS

In this part, you will learn the most fundamental aspects of protecting your security and privacy on the World Wide Web. These are the minimum measures that you must take when using the Internet.

→ Chapter 2: Risks at a Glance

→ Chapter 3: Importance of Good Passwords and Passphrases

→ Chapter 4: Avoiding Identity Theft

→ Chapter 5: Social Networking Sites and Online Forums

→ Chapter 6: Protecting Yourself from Malware

→ Chapter 7: Basic Windows Security

→ Chapter 8: Using Firewall Software

→ Chapter 9: Dangers of Wireless Networks and "Hotspots"

Chapter 2: Risks at a Glance

The data on your computer and the information revealed by your online activities are a treasure trove for hackers, snoops, spammers, identity thieves and other troublemakers alike.

The risks to your on- and off-line privacy and security come in various shapes and sizes, but let's try to carve out some broad categories to help make the risk management process more manageable.

Malware

In this book the term **malware** is used to cover threats such as viruses, worms, Trojans, rootkits, email/web bugs, adware and spyware, all of which have been designed with a malicious intent. The lines between these variations of malicious programs are blurring all the time, so the catchall term malware will be used. In one way or another, they are all geared to harm your computer, varying from the mildly annoying to the theft of your credit card or banking information.

Cracked Passwords

Weak passwords are more easily cracked, even by the most novice hackers using tools widely available on the Internet. To make matters worse, if one of your account passwords is cracked, this can lead to your other accounts being compromised as well. Someone cracking your main email account may gain access to a number of other passwords contained in confirmation emails or by sending 'forgotten password' requests to these other account providers. How? Easy: once a hacker gains access to your main email account, he can scan your Inbox and folders and find information about other sites where you have accounts. Then, by making 'forgotten password' requests at those other sites, the hacker will receive emails with reset passwords or instructions on how to create a new password.

Shared Networks; Sniffing

The more the world goes wireless and adopts more broadband connections, the more you are sharing network bandwidth with others. If your network or computer is not set up properly, third parties may be able to access your computer files or piggy-back on the bandwidth that you are paying for, perhaps even launching attacks on other victims under the guise of your Internet connection. Sophisticated hackers - called **sniffers** - can even pull your wirelessly transmitted information right out of the air.

Online Tracking; Profiling

As more and more aspects of people's lives migrate online, it is becoming easier for big business, spammers and hackers to collect and aggregate your online activities and preferences. By matching this information to a user's unique Internet fingerprint - something called an Internet Protocol address (or IP address for short) - vast, accurate and potentially intrusive personalized profiles are being amassed, including possibly yours.

More About: IP address

IP address stands for Internet Protocol address - a unique, numerical string of numbers, such as 123.456.78.90, that identifies every computer connected to the Internet.

Physical Security

Millions of computers and laptops are stolen every year. Computers often contain mountains of personal information and financial data. Why should an identity thief go to the trouble of trying to infiltrate your computer with complex methods when he can simply steal your laptop when you let your guard down at the local coffee shop? There are also less widely known privacy and security risks posed by photocopiers and printers too.

Scams; Spoofing; Phishing

Hackers will set up fake websites or send fake emails (methods known as **spoofing**) in order to pose as legitimate businesses to try and get you to click on or download malware. Other times they will use these spoofing techniques as a way to try and obtain your passwords or other sensitive personal or financial information (methods known as **phishing**). Sometimes these scams are easy to spot, but they are getting more and more sophisticated all the time.

Spam

Spam is usually associated with unsolicited commercial email, but spammers are now expanding these same techniques to newsgroups, chat, torrent and peer-to-peer media downloads. Spam is usually more annoying than dangerous unless it contains or transports malware, but even "harmless" spam wastes your time and bandwidth.

Adversaries

Much fuss is made (including in this book!) about hackers, snoops and identity thieves, but you must also be mindful of other potential adversaries that may wish to access your computer or learn about your online habits in order to harm you. These could include rival co-workers, jilted lovers, or any person with a grudge against you. Lawyers often advise clients to collect emails, transcripts of online chats, and cell phone text messages as part of their preparations for legal proceedings (e.g., employment claims, divorce or civil suits).

But don't despair! You can address and mitigate all of these risks. However, even this brief list should illustrate that it is not all smooth sailing on the Internet.

Chapter 3: Importance of Good Passwords and Passphrases

What Makes a Good Passphrase

Please note that in order to emphasize the techniques outlined in this chapter, the term **passphrase** is used as much as possible throughout this book instead of **password**. The term pass*word* denotes using a single word to protect against third parties gaining unauthorized access to your information. To better protect your information, you should use longer, more complex constructions - a pass*phrase* - to safeguard against any unauthorized access.

Simply stated: you must use strong passphrases! This is one of the most fundamental aspects to your security. Your information is only as secure as the passphrases you use to protect it.

A **weak** passphrase is anything that:

- is less than 7 characters long

- contains your name or any proper nouns, or

- does not have a mix of at least 3 character types (i.e., alpha uppercase, alpha lowercase, numeric). You should also use symbols (e.g., ! - ⌐), if possible.

In order to protect yourself from "brute force" dictionary attacks, use a variety of **alpha characters** of varying cases, **numerical** and **symbolic characters**. Do not use your name, license plate number, bankcard PIN number, favorite movie, family birth dates or anything else that is personal to you.

Pick something random and even ridiculous. If you follow these guidelines, a brute force or dictionary attack will simply take too long to overcome your passphrase protection. The snoops will move on to an easier victim.

More About: Brute Force or Dictionary Attacks

A brute force or dictionary attack is a method that hackers use to defeat security measures by trying all possible dictionary terms to resolve a password or passphrase. In particular, the hackers use a software program to try every word in the dictionary, as well as combinations and variants of the words, as possible passphrases to gain entry into your accounts. This hacking method can be amazingly simple and fast, and can give hackers access to your accounts in a short amount of time.

Also important: do not note down your passphrases anywhere! This includes keeping them on a USB stick (unless you have encrypted it using strong encryption - see 'Chapter 13: Encrypting Your Files to Keep them Safe' starting on page 161).

Although somewhat kitschy, think of passphrases a bit like your underpants: change them often, only use your own, keep them hidden and out of sight, do not share them with anyone including your friends, and do not leave them lying around in plain view.

Of course, you should apply common sense when it comes to passphrases. You may not always need super complicated passphrases for websites that, for example, do not have any of your confidential or sensitive information such as your bank credit card or social insurance numbers.

To keep the number of passphrases that you must remember to a manageable level you might use the same passphrase for accounts that do *not* include sensitive information and use complicated passphrases for accounts that do contain your important data.

Do be careful applying such "common sense" however because it may be possible for a hacker to discover sensitive information indirectly from your non-sensitive accounts (see the paragraph below about *knock-on security risks* in the section 'Different Passphrases for Different Accounts' below).

Automatically Generate a Strong Passphrase

If you have trouble coming up with your own good passphrases, there are plenty of websites and tools to help you, including:

- the passphrase generator on the PCTools.com website is simple to use - http://www.pctools.com/guides/password/

- Bytes Interactive's passphrase generator is also handy - http://www.goodpassword.com/

- (for Advanced Users) Ultra High Security Password Generator (very long and complex passphrases) - https://www.grc.com/passwords.htm

Once you generate a passphrase, you can use Microsoft's Password Checker to check the strength of it - https://www.microsoft.com/security/pc-security/password-checker.aspx

Different Passphrases for Different Accounts

It is also recommended that you use a unique passphrase for each online account. Otherwise, your online account security is only as good as your weakest passphrase.

For example, computer forensic experts are trained to 'crack the easy passwords first' because many people use the same or similar passphrases for all of their passphrase needs. Hackers and snoops similarly exploit the fact that many people repeat the same passphrase or only alter them slightly each time. Also, your employer or colleagues may have access to some of your passphrases; if you use this same passphrase for any other accounts, they could be compromised.

Such **knock-on security risks** can also arise when a hacker gains access to a non-sensitive account and then uses the information he finds there to correctly guess or crack your more sensitive accounts. For example, a hacker may be able to obtain your passphrase by accessing the site's 'forgotten password' feature and take a chance answering the security questions using little more information than your birth date, your mother's maiden name or the name of your pet. Perhaps the hacker has gleaned this information from posts, including your own, on a social networking site. If the hacker was to gain access to your main email account, he could access past confirmation emails you received from other online sign-ups that contain even more usernames and passphrases. Or the hacker could send 'forgotten password' requests from your main email account. In addition, it is almost certain that the hacker would immediately change your mail passphrase and thereby lock you out.

Using Tools to Keep Track of Your Passphrases

Although not the recommended best practice, if you have difficulty remembering many passphrases, some aides may help you.

RoboForm at http://ww.roboform.com/ is a popular and reliable passphrase manager, but many other programs exist, including some free ones. A good collection of passphrase manager software is found at http://download.cnet.com/windows/password-managers/.

LastPass Password Manager at http://lastpass.com/ is a handy passphrase management tool for all your online accounts which supports most browsers. You set up one master passphrase with LastPass and from there it keeps and manages all of the passphrases for your online accounts. LastPass will also help you devise strong passphrases. The underlying data is kept on LastPass' encrypted servers - hence, using this service requires a degree of trust in the provider - but this allows you to access your passphrases remotely from any computer with Internet access.

Chapter 4: Avoiding Identity Theft

Introduction

You've probably read stories about **identity theft**; a crime that Gallup says is more prevalent in the US than burglary, mugging, car theft and physical assault *combined*. So what is identity theft, and how can you avoid falling victim to it? Identity theft happens when somebody uses your personal information or username and passphrases to impersonate you.

The main problem is that the process of identity theft can start with only a few pieces of information such as your name, address, phone number, banking data, social security number, or similar personally-identifiable information. Once someone steals your identity, they might be able to withdraw your money, use your identity to take out mortgages and loans, or even commit fraud by signing up for services, government hand-outs and credit cards in your name.

On average it takes more than *twelve months* for a person to realize that their identity has been stolen. By then, much damage may already have been done to their reputation and credit rating. It can also take a long time to undo the damage caused by identity theft, so it's important to take proactive steps to protect yourself from identity thieves.

Protecting Yourself from Phishing Attacks

One way that identity thieves try to get access to your personal information is through a scam called **phishing** (pronounced fishing). Phishing is where somebody pretends to be an organization such as your bank or an online shop, and uses a fake email or a fake web page to trick you into providing your username, passphrase or personal information. **Spear phishing** refers to highly targeted phishing attempts where, for example, the fake emails are specifically addressed to you and therefore seem all the more legitimate. Sometimes phishing scams are easily spotted, but other times it is almost impossible to tell the difference between fake and legitimate websites.

To make sure you are dealing with a legitimate website, you should pay close attention to the URL (website address) displayed in your browser's address bar. Phishers will often include part of a legitimate website's name in the link that they are trying to trick you to click on (e.g., http://cogipas.example.com/) so take a close second look. To make matters worse, the URL you see in an HTML-based email message or on a web page is not necessarily the true destination of the link. If you use your mouse to hover over the link without clicking on it, many email software and web browsers will display the link's true URL, either in a small, pop-up display or in the status bar at the bottom left of the application's window. Make sure that the true link looks valid before you click on it.

Look out too for the tone of the message. Many phishing emails attempt to scare you into logging in to your account immediately, so you do not take the time to notice that the site is fake. They'll often threaten to deactivate your account, suggest you've got a large unexpected bill to pay, or say your account has been hacked.

Most banks do not include any links in their email messages to you. Instead, they ask you to go to your browser and type in their domain name, which you can check on your bank statement or any paperwork from the bank. By manually typing in the address of the website you want to visit in your browser this means even if you receive a phishing email and react to it, you'll end up at the real bank's website in any event, so no damage will be done.

You should use the same technique of typing the URL directly into your browser rather than clicking on it even if a friend or other trusted source sends you a link to a website you know. The email may have come from a trusted source, but perhaps they have fallen victim to malware or their system was compromised. It's always better to be safe than sorry. Otherwise, you may not notice that the link is to www.c0gipas.com (rather than www.cogipas.com) and that you are falling for a fake phishing site. And even this technique will not be entirely foolproof if, for example, the underlying URL has been compromised.

Many web browsers, email clients and webmail services offer **phishing filters**. These help like spam filters in preventing phishing emails from ever reaching your Inbox. Although the filters are not foolproof, they are yet one more layer of protection in your lines of defense. Use them!

If You Get Phished In

If you do fall for a phishing scam and enter your details into a fake site, go to the legitimate site and change your passphrase *immediately*. If the hacker beats you to it, he could lock you out of your own account and **hijack** it. To make matters worse and as previously mentioned, if your email account is compromised, the hacker may then be able to find out about your other accounts from confirmation emails in your archives or start to make 'forgotten password' requests under your name in order to obtain them.

If you are locked out it can be difficult indeed to get your account back. You can't just solve it with an email to the site's helpdesk saying your account was hijacked and you want it back. If it were that easy, this is a technique that the hackers would use to seize control of your account in the first place.

To help ensure that others do not fall for the same phishing attack, you could also report the incident to the Anti-Phishing Working Group (APWG) at http://www.antiphishing.org/. There may be no immediate personal benefit in reporting a phishing attempt, but it will help in the overall fight to reduce the number of people getting swindled.

If you do become a victim of outright identity theft, you should report the matter to the FTC at https://www.ftccomplaintassistant.gov/. While the FTC will *not* resolve your individual consumer complaints, they will use the information to help in the pursuit of prosecutions and investigations as well as to detect patterns of unlawful activity.

As you can probably detect, you may have a long, hard, lonely slog to reverse the damage caused by the identity thieves. This is why *prevention* is so important.

Protecting Yourself from Keyloggers

Keylogging is another way hackers steal sensitive information. This involves a hacker, without your knowledge, installing software on your computer that captures the key presses on your computer keyboard and sends them to the hacker. Needless to say, in no time the hacker will have the usernames and passphrases for a number of your online accounts. Sometimes the keylogging software is installed using a virus or Trojan (for more about what these are, please see 'Chapter 6: Protecting Yourself from Malware' on page 33).

Some employers also use keylogging to monitor their employees. In addition, computer forensic experts are trained to install keyloggers, including in advance of a computer being seized, in order to capture as much information, including passphrases, as possible.

There are also *physical* keyloggers which are small hardware devices discreetly attached between your keyboard and the port at the back of your computer. Physical keyloggers require that the hacker have direct access to your computer, but such keyloggers are not detectible by anti-malware software.

You can thwart keylogging with a number of tools, including SpyCop at http://www.spycop.com/. It detects if any keylogging programs or any keylogging type activities are present on your system, and will purge them for you.

Understanding Credit Reports and Data Brokers

Credit reports provide a central repository of your financial health, so that when you request a loan, a bank can see what other loans you already have and can make sure you can afford it. In many jurisdictions, you are entitled to access your credit report (sometimes free or for a nominal fee) and to correct any errors. This sounds easy. The *requesting* part of the process usually is straightforward, but *correcting* erroneous information can be an uphill struggle at times. So be prepared to be persistent.

Of course, credit reports can be used legitimately by banks (to approve loans), potential employers (as part of background checks), or lawyers (for due diligence checks). There can be important consequences to any erroneous information appearing in these databases. For this reason, you should check the most important ones (see below) regularly - annually for example - and tenaciously correct any errors you do find.

Periodically checking your files is also a good way to detect any strange activity that suggests you may have been a victim of identity theft.

Each company has its own policies regarding how you access and correct the information they have on file about you. Follow their directions meticulously; otherwise, they may use the slightest excuse not to comply.

Checking Your Record with Credit Reporting Agencies

There are three main credit reporting agencies. You should request and check the information held by *all three* because the information on file may differ between them. You can start checking your record by visiting their websites, noted here:

> **Equifax** - www.equifax.com
>
> **Experian** - www.experian.com
>
> **TransUnion** - www.transunion.com

Checking Other Sources

Although not among the 'big three' credit reporting houses above, you may also want to check what **Innovis** and **PRBC/Microbilt** have on file about you as they too build up credit reports. If you do find something amiss in your report, both websites contain information and contact details about how to have the information corrected.

To access your credit report from **Innovis**, go to:

> https://www.innovis.com/InnovisWeb/pers_orderCreditReport.html
> (or go to www.innovis.com > Personal Services > Order Your Innovis Credit Report)

For **Microbilt**, go to:

> http://www.microbilt.com/consumer-dispute.aspx
> (or go to http://www.microbilt.com/ and type "disputes" in the Search box)

The **MIB Group** also maintains consumer files, but related to health- and medical-insurance information. At the time of writing, to request your consumer file for free from MIB you can go straight to:

> http://www.mib.com/html/request_your_record.html
> (or go to www.mib.com > Consumers > Request Your MIB Consumer File)

Another large source of database information is **Lexis-Nexis** which caters to attorneys and related clients. Lexis-Nexis does permit you to **opt-out** from their database (your ability to opt-out may vary), technically called a *request for suppression*. For more information, visit:

http://www.lexisnexis.com/privacy/for-consumers/opt-out-of-lexisnexis.aspx
(should this URL change type "lexis nexis opt-out" in your favorite search engine)

Identity Theft Prevention Checklist - How to Protect Yourself

To protect yourself from identity theft, you need to put measures in place that make life hard for identity thieves. Like the defences of a castle, you must set up a number of layers of protection. Use this checklist to make sure you are protected. Check the detailed explanations cross-referenced elsewhere in this book.

- ✓ Use strong passphrases for your email and online accounts (see 'Chapter 3: Importance of Good Passwords and Passphrases' on page 23)

- ✓ Always keep your operating system and anti-malware software up-to-date (see 'Chapter 6: Protecting Yourself from Malware' on page 33)

- ✓ Securely set up your wireless network (see 'Chapter 9: Dangers of Wireless Networks and "Hotspots"' on page 63)

- ✓ Don't access password protected sites on an unknown or public computer (such as a library terminal or at an Internet café)

- ✓ Be wary of public Internet hot spots such as the wireless Internet access zones at airports (see 'Using Hotspots Securely' on page 70)

- ✓ Don't click on attachments or links, or visit websites, or reply to emails that seem in any way suspicious (see 'Typing Email Links into Your Browser' on page 43)

- ✓ Don't post personal information on online forums or social networking sites (see 'Chapter 5: Social Networking Sites and Online Forums on page 33)

- ✓ Don't provide sensitive information - especially passphrases - by unencrypted email or chat or by telephone (see 'Scams; Spoofing; Phishing' on page 22 and 'Chapter 15: Using Email, Webmail and Remailers' on page 199)

- ✓ Encrypt the sensitive files on your computer (see 'Chapter 13: Encrypting Your Files to Keep them Safe' starting on page 161)

- ✓ Delete sensitive information properly from your computer by wiping it (see 'Chapter 14: Wiping Your Sensitive Data' on page 173)

- ✓ Encrypt your email and other electronic communications (see 'Chapter 15: Using Email, Webmail and Remailers' on page 199)

✓ Check your credit reports regularly (see the 'Checking Your Record with Credit Reporting Agencies' section above)

More Resources

One of the best sources of information about identity theft is the US government's central website, http://www.ftc.gov/bcp/edu/microsites/idtheft/.

The US Federal Trade Commission also maintains information about how you can obtain your credit report for free from each credit reporting agency once per year. See http://www.ftc.gov/freereports and http://www.ftc.gov/bcp/edu/pubs/consumer/credit/cre34.shtm.

Chapter 5: Social Networking Sites and Online Forums

Introduction

Social networking sites (sometimes called *social networks*) and other online forums are a great way to get back in touch with people and to make new friends - whether buddies from high school or the neighbor down the street. Everyone and their mother (make that grandma even) seem to be on Facebook and Google+ nowadays. The same holds true for online forums - these are fantastic resources to get information, read fan fiction or to just chat with people from across the globe that have the same interests as you.

But, as you know by now, online is not synonymous with safe. There are a number of risks associated with being active on social networking sites and online forums.

Understanding the Risks

It is often said that if an Internet service is free, you are not the customer, you are the product. It is wise to keep this maxim in mind especially for social networking sites and online forums.

Assume that Blog Entries are Forever

It is easy and tempting to blog and post about your personal life. But with social networking sites and online forums, the information you blog about may spread beyond your control and could be used by unscrupulous marketers to track your behavior or build a profile about you. In combination with other tactics used by commercial interests that are described in this book, like IP address tracking and employing email/web bugs, the marketers could build an astonishingly detailed profile about you that could be used, shared and built upon for years to come.

Information you blogged/tweeted about or put on someone's Facebook wall could also come back to haunt you in other ways, by affecting academic admissions, career prospects and personal relationships.

It is no longer difficult to imagine a job applicant or political candidate being probed about a blog entry or post on a social networking site from earlier days. More and more big corporations also harvest personal and sensitive data about potential and current employees from the Internet. You have no way of knowing what is being recorded in databases and by whom.

Your Social Media Presence is not Wholly within Your own Control

Have you ever had someone tag a picture on Facebook with your name? This happens often and can quickly become annoying. You have little control over what is posted about you in this fashion by other users on their walls. These posts can be narratives that mention your name or can be images that identify you in the tags. Worst of all, the risk of people posting about you exists even if you do not have your own account on the social networking site!

Other threats include phishing attempts, Trojans and worm-like hazards that are specifically designed to target social networking sites (Koobface was one such example), and so on. Facebook, Google+ and other social networking sites have become adept at acting quickly in the face of such threats, but as a user, you should do all you can to protect yourself.

Scarier risks, though thankfully more remote, include those of cyber-bullying, cyber-stalking or worse.

How to Stay Safe

Settings and Good Habits

Double-check your privacy settings on the social networking sites and online forums you participate in to ensure that your profile is *not* shared with the public at large. For instance, log out of your social networking site and then type your name in your favorite search engine. Do not be surprised if your social networking profile turns up in the search results - click on it and check what information is displayed on the page and thus generally available to the public. This is the information a virtual stranger anywhere on the globe can access about you. If all your contact information, family photos and wall posts are visible, it's time you changed your privacy settings.

In addition, it is better to err on the side of caution and keep your circle of friends or buddies as small as possible. Some people get a kick out of having hundreds of friends or buddies displayed on their profile, but unless you truly do have hundreds of genuine admirers this is probably a mistake. Be selective with your invites, and focus on quality over quantity.

If you do have hundreds of friends, relatives and admirers, is it absolutely necessary that all of them should be able to access the same information? Most social networking sites, Facebook and Google+ included, have handy tools that let you filter who does and who does not see your information, even *among* your friends. Use these settings to create different sub-lists or circles of people who can see all your information, and others who see a more limited subset of your posted materials.

What Never to Post

Given the open and fun nature of social networking sites and online forums, it is all too easy to let your guard down with the kind of information you post. Regardless of how careful you are with your privacy settings and limiting access to your profile and pages, NEVER post the following information:

- your date of birth

- your address

- your phone number

- your middle name

- your picture

- your vacation or away plans

- any similar information about friends and family members

In official speak this category of information is sometimes referred to as **sensitive unclassified information**. Identity thieves could use such details to reassemble and assume your identity. Old fashioned thieves could use your away plans to conduct a hassle-free robbery (see the now defunct http://pleaserobme.com/ which aptly made this point and caused a stir).

People find the recommendation not to post your picture difficult to accept, but with the introduction and growing use of facial recognition technology, this recommendation is more important than ever.

Do everything you can to make sure these golden nuggets of personal information do not enter the public domain. Once "out there" you never know who may be collecting and trading or sharing in your information or when this might come back to haunt you.

Don't Implicate Yourself, Dummy

There are regularly stories about people posting information to a social networking site or a forum which is later used to implicate them in a scandal. This can lead to workplace discipline, academic sanctions, matrimonial agony, risking a security clearance, and overall reduced future prospects in your personal and professional life.

Some users also have a habit of sharing too much about their employer online - information about reorganizations, hirings or firings, products or projects. This can lead to consequences for you and your employer - ranging from just embarrassing to legal problems. If you're the spouse of an employee and you tweeted about the long hours your spouse is spending on Project X, you could be in this category too.

As a general, but all too often ignored, rule: **pause** and **use common sense** before posting anything potentially scandalous online. Keep in mind that it may be virtually impossible to un-do the post and that it may take on a life of its own; so make sure you can live with all of your posts for years to come.

If something damning about you is posted, either by you or someone else, do try and engage in some **wall scrubbing**. This can take many forms and includes when you quickly try to undo or delete your own posts, request others to do the same with their posts, or ask the service itself to remove the information (sometimes by you **flagging** the post as inappropriate). Obviously, the time and difficulty involved in these efforts increases in the same order as they are listed. Even if the information is removed, it may already have been picked up by others, re-posted or picked up in automated feeds or search engine caches, thereby making it difficult indeed to get the genie back in the bottle.

Think Before Clicking on Links

Hoaxes and fake messages that lead to pages and applications (or apps) that are trying to sell you something abound on social networking sites. Such links could purportedly come from friends, but remember: hackers can get into social networking accounts and send fake or malicious information to everyone in their victims' friends lists. If something looks suspicious or too good to be true, it probably is. Don't click on links or, at the very least, if you are suspicious ask the sender if they sent it and if the information is legitimate before you do.

Chapter 6: Protecting Yourself from Malware

What is Malware?

As used in this book, malicious software (or **malware** for short) collectively means viruses, worms, Trojans, rootkits, email/web bugs, adware and spyware.

Malware spreads in many ways including email (both as links and attachments), malicious websites (whether as pop-up windows or code embedded in web pages) and, of course, downloads (whether via the web, torrent/P2P, chat or newsgroups).

In addition to being disruptive and a nuisance, malware can be used to steal your personal data or turn your computer into a **zombie**. A zombie is a computer that has been taken over and is controlled remotely, and which is sometimes used for illegal acts.

Below, each category of malware is described in more detail. However, the lines between these categories are blurring more and more as the malware and their creators get more sophisticated in their methods.

What is a Virus?

A computer **virus** is a software program (a piece of executable code) that is capable of replicating itself and wreaking havoc on your files and data. Such programs are usually created with malicious intent. A typical virus operates on your computer without your knowledge or permission. It first attaches itself to a file or program on your computer. When the infected program runs, the virus multiplies itself and infects other files or programs on the same computer as well as on other computers that are connected through a network to the original computer.

A virus spreads when an infected file is sent through a removable medium such as a USB stick, portable drive, CD, DVD, Blu-Ray disc, floppy disk, through a network file system or the Internet. Among these, the Internet is the most prevalent medium nowadays. Viruses can be sent as email attachments in the form of images, greeting cards, audio files or video files. When you double-click on an infected attachment, it surreptitiously infects your computer. Many viruses are also capable of using email programs to spread themselves to other computers (see 'What is a Worm' below). Viruses can also be spread through instant messaging programs.

The damage caused by a computer virus can be serious. It can corrupt or change data or even delete everything on your hard drive. It can forge your email address and send mails to all the contacts in your address book. Sometimes, it may just multiply itself without causing any damage to the files, but even in such a minor case, it still degrades the performance of your system by utilizing resources such as memory or drive space. Once infected, your computer may run slowly, often lock up, have corrupt applications or crash.

Viruses come in all shapes and sizes. For example, a *boot sector virus* infects the boot record of your hard drive. When you boot (start-up) the infected computer, it infects other removable media used by the computer including USB sticks and portable drives. *File infector viruses* infect executable program files (e.g., *.EXE, *.COM) and some may persist in memory and thus keep infecting other files. *Macro viruses* infect data files such as documents, spreadsheets, presentations or database files (e.g., *.DOC, *.XLS, *.PPT, *.ADP). *Multi-partite* is a fancy name for a virus that combines two or more of these virus types.

What is a Worm?

A **worm** is very similar to a virus in that it is a malicious software program. However, it differs in that a worm reproduces and spreads *automatically* from computer to computer.

Similar to other malware, worms can make their way into your system through email attachments, links to websites with malicious content or executable scripts. The moment you click on the attachment, link or otherwise activate the malicious content, the worm installs itself into your system.

Once a worm is installed on your system, it usually locates your address book and without your knowledge sends every one of your contacts an email with the same attachment or link to the original worm. The worm then sends similar emails to everyone listed in those recipients' address books and so on; the process can go on for some time! A worm uses up computer time and network bandwidth in this way, making your system slow or unresponsive. It may also open **ports** on your computer (see the 'Ports Explained - An Introduction' section starting on page 59) to create network security holes through which hackers can install a backdoor in your system. Your computer could then become a zombie under the hacker's control.

Apart from creating network damage, a worm can also damage your computer like a virus. It can corrupt or delete crucial system files and even stop some critical programs from working.

What is a Trojan?

Similar to the legendary horse given by the Greeks to the people of Troy, the term **Trojan** describes a malicious software program that poses as a legitimate or a useful application. The moment you click on it, it gets installed and begins its malicious action without your knowledge. In contrast to a computer virus, generally a Trojan cannot replicate or infect other files. When detected, Trojans should be deleted.

A Trojan may arrive as an attachment to emails or be part of a software download from websites or peer-to-peer (P2P) file sharing networks or any other way you obtain downloads. For example, a Trojan may introduce itself by posing as an anti-malware program. Most Trojans have file extension *.EXE (an *executable* file meaning a file that you can run), but may be disguised and named to look like a game, movie or a music download. Because Windows may hide the file's extension by default, users may think or be tricked into thinking that the download is a non-executable file (please see the 'Don't Hide Your File Extensions' section on page 44).

There are many different categories of Trojans. A *Remote Access Trojan* (RAT) gives an attacker absolute control over your computer. The attacker can access your personal information like credit card numbers, passwords and financial documents stored in your computer. A *Keylogging Trojan* can log your keystrokes both online and offline and email a log file to the attacker on a regular basis. The attacker can then retrieve sensitive information such as passwords from the logs. A *Destructive Trojan* can destroy data files and core system files of your computer, while a *Software Detection Killer Trojan* can kill the anti-malware and firewall programs on your computer making it vulnerable. An *IRC Trojan* uses Internet Relay Chat servers (a type of Internet chat discussed in Chapter 17) to route the attacker's commands to compromised computers.

Windows-based systems are usually the most vulnerable to Trojan attacks due to their popularity and, according to some commentators, the security loopholes in this family of operating system.

What is a Rootkit?

A **rootkit** is a collection of programs used to obtain and maintain undetected administrative level access to your computer. It modifies specific code in the operating system and becomes part of the operating system, thus ensuring that your anti-malware software cannot detect the rootkit.

A rootkit can ride piggyback on software that looks legitimate. It may also be acquired from shared disks and drives, infected web content or via malicious email links. It propagates itself using a blended threat mechanism which is a combination of the dropper, the loader and the rootkit. The *dropper* gets into your computer using any of the posing methods mentioned previously. The *loader* is launched when you click the malicious link or software and then loads the rootkit into your system's memory.

A rootkit mainly creates a "backdoor" into your computer that can be used by hackers to hide their spyware, viruses and Trojans from anti-malware and system management utilities. With "administrator" level access (i.e., full, unfettered access to your computer), the hackers can execute files, access logs, monitor your activities, change your computer configuration and attack other machines on the network virtually undetected.

Certain sophisticated rootkits - called *kernel mode rootkits* - can directly "conquer" the operating system and modify data structures on the kernel (i.e., the heart of your computer's operating system). For example, the rootkit could remove itself from the list of activities on your system, making it difficult for you even to detect it.

A rootkit can target many operating systems like Linux, Mac or Windows. Normally, you will have to completely delete your computer's hard drive and reinstall the operating system if you detect a rootkit on your system.

What is an Email Bug or Web Bug?

Email bugs or **web bugs** are actually invisibly small or transparent images embedded in an email or a web page that are served (displayed) from a remote, third party location. When you open the HTML-based email or access the web page, the presence of the bug essentially reports this action back to a third party server, allowing that party to track when you opened the email or page and even why you may have done so (e.g., to respond to a related advertisement or promotion).

Marketers may also use email/web bugs to record and track your IP address for profiling purposes. For example, if a business uses its website's cookies in tandem with email bugs, that business could 'match' your IP address with your email address and build a sophisticated profile about you.

If you use web mail, you may have noticed that your provider may *block images* from displaying in your email unless you specifically choose to allow them. This is the mail provider's attempt to shield you from email bugs.

What are Adware and Spyware?

Adware and **spyware** run in the background of your system, sometimes constantly, eating up your computer's memory and processing power, all the while logging your activities and sometimes even sending these records to a remote location, either in real-time or at regular intervals.

Adware and spyware are not always easily distinguished and another reason why this book includes them in the broad definition of malware. **Adware** is usually installed with your agreement (though sometimes you are tricked into it) and can usually be *un*installed like any normal software. On the other hand, **spyware** is installed more stealthily, sometimes disguised entirely as something else, without your knowledge or agreement and may be difficult to uninstall.

Are You Infected?

The "symptoms" of your computer being compromised by malware vary. Sometimes your computer will begin acting strangely, start to freeze and crash regularly or run more slowly, or perhaps its hard drive keeps whirring away even though you are not running any programs.

The best thing to do if you think you are infected is to perform a **full scan** of all files with your updated anti-malware software, even if this means running it overnight.

Top Tip

Some malware loads up at the earliest stages of your computer's start up, so to be extra cautious, you can run your anti-malware check after booting into Windows Safe Mode. You can boot into Safe Mode usually by pressing F8 just before Windows tries to start. Booting into Safe Mode ensures that a minimum of processes are running when you perform a malware scan.

In addition to scanning your computer regularly with your anti-malware software, Microsoft also maintains a free malware detection and removal tool which is regularly updated and available for download at http://www.microsoft.com/security/malwareremove/default.aspx.

What's Running on Your System?

It is not always easy to determine if something suspicious is running on your computer, especially if it is something running in the background. You can investigate a little bit with Windows Task Manager. Type "task manager" in your Windows Start menu and select the item **View running processes with Task Manager** (this is shown below).

Figure: Starting Windows Task Manager

Once in Task Manager, you can view what applications, processes and services are running by selecting the appropriate tab. To see the processes running on your system, click on the 'Processes' tab (see the next screenshot).

Then click on the 'Memory' column to sort the processes by those using the most amount of memory. These are not always easy to understand, but may provide clues as to what may be slowing down your system. If any process looks suspicious or out of place, including by the amount of memory it is using, perform a search about it in your favorite search engine, but only rely on the information you find from *reputable* sources. You should never "kill" a process (by clicking on the 'End Process' button after selecting the process) unless you are confident about what you are doing.

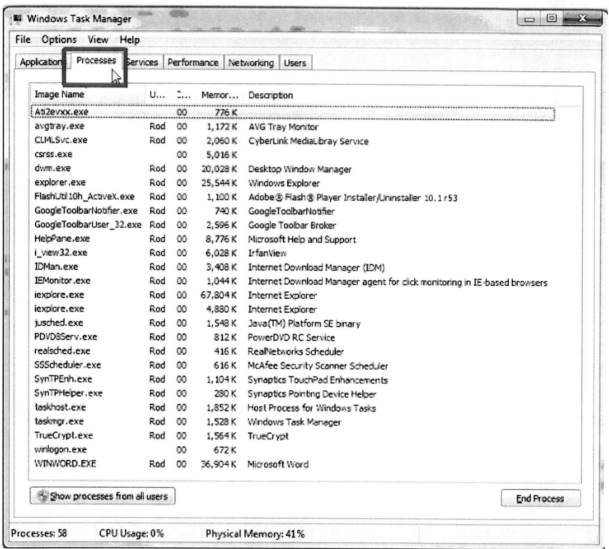

Figure: The Processes tab of the Windows Task Manager

The next tab after Processes, Services, are a bit more complicated and covered at the end of this chapter starting on page 46.

Using Anti-malware Software

The single best way to protect yourself from malware is to have up-to-date anti-malware software. Some software comes as comprehensive package covering viruses, adware and spyware in the same module alike, while other packages come in separate modules.

Because malware and the hackers that use them are always adapting and changing, you should always keep your defenses up-to-date by regularly downloading the latest "virus definitions" for your malware software. These definitions are the databases that help your malware software identity malware and malware-like activity or symptoms in the first place. Keeping your definitions up-to-date can usually be set automatically and the more frequently you update them the better.

Recommended Anti-malware Software

AVG Anti-Virus Free Edition at http://free.avg.com/ is a good anti-virus (and anti-adware/spyware) package that deserves its popularity. AVG is a good combination of simple, powerful and hassle-free. An upgrade to the "complete" package also offers a decent firewall, but see the excellent free options for firewall software in 'Chapter 8: Using Firewall Software' starting on page 57.

Don't Surf as an Administrator

This tip may not appeal to advanced users, but consider surfing the Internet with a Windows user account of **limited privileges**. In Windows-speak, this means logging on to Windows with a non-administrator account before surfing the Internet. If malware attacks your computer when you are signed in with a limited user account, there is much less damage the attack can inflict.

Even if this tip does not appeal to you personally (as you are a 'power user' and, for example, want the ability to install software) set up **limited accounts** for your children or guests using your computer.

Typing Email Links into Your Browser

When you receive an email containing a link, rather than clicking on the link, *type* the address manually into your web browser. This is especially recommended - even mandatory - for emails that you were not expecting or are from unknown sources. It is easy to be fooled into clicking on a link that sends you to a fake or spoofed website. These links can look convincing. Instead, if you type the link into your browser, you will never be tricked into visiting www.amaz0n.com or www.facebok.com when you wanted www.amazon.com or www.facebook.com. (As it happens, both of these misspellings will take you to the proper sites, but that is not always the case.)

More About: Phishing

Phishing is where a malicious website may try to pass itself off as a legitimate site - sometimes with a similar-looking domain name and sign-in page - in an attempt to fool you into providing your username and passphrase, or perhaps even your credit card details, address, or other personal information.

Using Spam Filters

Spam filters - filters that prevent you from receiving unsolicited junk email - are widely available for most email software and webmail providers. Enabling these filters and spending some time with the settings should help prevent a lot of spam and malware from reaching your Inbox in the first place.

Don't Hide Your File Extensions

When you double-click on a file, Windows knows which program to open it with because of the file's **extension** (usually three letters after the last dot in a filename, such as *.DOC). By default or at other times, Windows may hide your file extensions. When hidden, this means that Windows will not display the extensions of files that are associated with an application.

Hiding file extensions can be dangerous because this makes it easier for hackers to masquerade malicious files as innocuous ones. For example, KISS_ME.JPG.exe will look like a harmless picture file if the extension is hidden, but it is actually a potentially dangerous executable file. Please look at it again.

Another example is if you received or downloaded the file BEAUTIFUL.AVI.vbs. If your settings were set to hide extensions, it would display as BEAUTIFUL.AVI. You might be tempted to click on it (especially if it was sent by a friend) and expect to see a video. However, the extension is actually *.VBS and the file an executable type of scripting language that could be used to harm your computer. There are dozens of executable file types (comprehensive listings can be found by typing "executable file types" in your favorite search engine), but the most common are *.BAT, *.COM, *.EXE, *.PIF, *.SCR, *.REG, *.VB and *.VBS.

It is important that you do *not* hide your extensions because some malware distribution scams take advantage of this. If you keep file extensions in plain view, the scenarios above will be more apparent to you and you will be less likely to be tricked into double-clicking on similar potential (hidden) threats.

To make sure that your file extensions are *not* hidden follow these steps. In **Windows Explorer**, select *Tools* > *Folder options...* (as shown in the next screenshot)

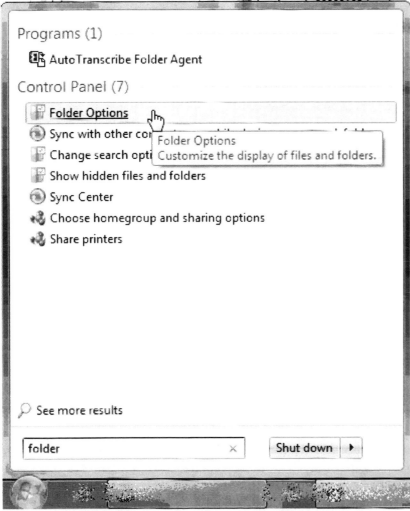

Figure: Accessing Folder Options in Windows Explorer

Alternatively, you can also access **Folder Options** directly in the Window Start menu (shown below).

Programs (1)

   AutoTranscribe Folder Agent

Control Panel (7)

   Folder Options

   Sync with other co...
   Folder Options
   Change search opti   Customize the display of files and folders.

   Show hidden files and folders

   Sync Center

   Choose homegroup and sharing options

   Share printers

   See more results

   folder   ×   Shut down ▶

Figure: Accessing Folder Options via the Windows Start menu

Once the Folder Options dialogue box opens, choose the **View** tab (see the next screenshot). Then, *de*select the **Hide extension for known file types** (make sure it is *not* selected and remains *un*checked) and click **OK**.

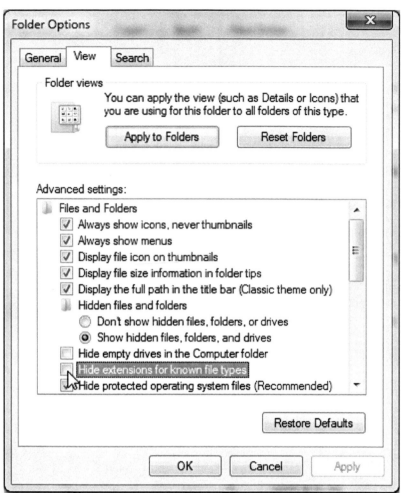

Figure: Making sure the hide extensions option is *un*checked

Windows should now always display file extensions and *not* hide them. This will help ensure that you are not fooled into clicking on dangerous attachments that are camouflaged to look like other files.

How to Check What Services are Running on Your System (Advanced Users)

As discussed earlier in this chapter, it is not always easy to determine if something suspicious is running on your computer, especially if it is running in the background. Earlier, you were shown how to investigate **Processes** with Windows Task Manager. Type "task manager" in your Windows Start menu and select **View running processes with Task Manager** (see the next screenshot).

Figure: Starting Task Manager

In Task Manager you can not only view what applications and processes are running, but you can also check on **Services** too by selecting the appropriate tab (see the next screenshot).

Services are not always easy to understand but may, in combination with some Internet research using your favorite search engine, provide clues as to what may be slowing down your system. In essence, services are programs that run quietly in the background of your system.

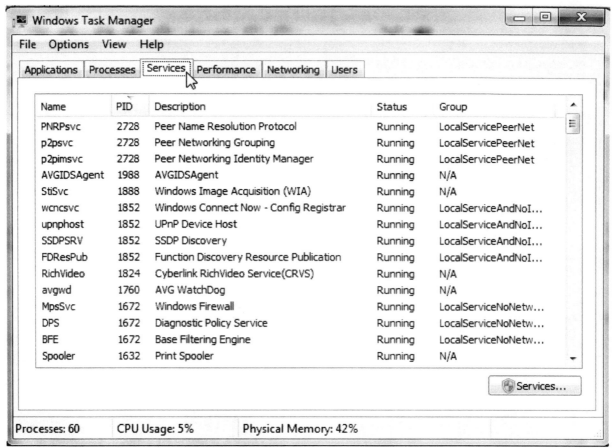

Figure: The Services tab of Task Manager

Under the Services tab, you can explore these a little more by selecting a certain entry and clicking on the **Services...** button at the lower right, and then exploring the individual services in the new window that opens.

Some services are rarely, if ever used, and others still may be completely unnecessary for your computer experience. There is plenty of advice on the Internet about what services are unnecessary - just type "which windows services should I disable" into your favorite search engine - but what is appropriate to disable varies from user to user. One thoughtful analysis is here, http://www.blackviper.com/Windows_7/servicecfg.htm.

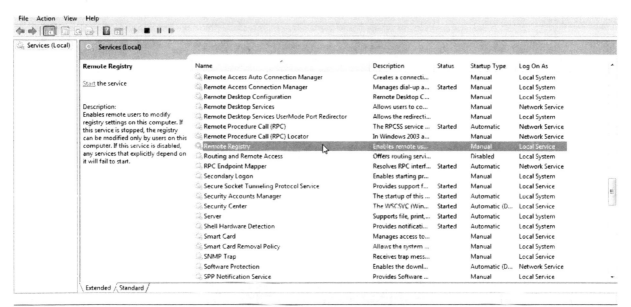

Figure: When you select a Service in the list you will see a brief description of its function displayed at the left

A few Services you could *consider* disabling include:

> **Offline Files** - You can safely disable this service if you do not synchronize files *between* computers.

> **Remote Registry** (the service selected in the screenshot above). This service allows a network administrator to change your system's Registry *remotely*, so there is virtually no reason for the average home user to need Remote Registry Service. See http://www.theeldergeek.com/remote_registry.htm.

> **Windows Media Player Network Sharing Service** - You can safely disable this service if you do not need to share Windows Media Player libraries to other networked players or media devices using Universal Plug and Play (UPnP). If you do not know what UPnP is, then you probably do not need it and can safely disable it.

> **Windows Search** - This is a resource intense service, so consider disabling it *unless* you often perform file searches.

Some users have disabled all of the above services on their computer(s) and noticed no ill effects.

Disabling a Service

To disable a service, select the service in the list (as shown in the previous screenshot), right-click and select **Properties**. In the resulting menu (shown in the screenshot below), under **Startup type:** choose *Disabled* and then click **OK**.

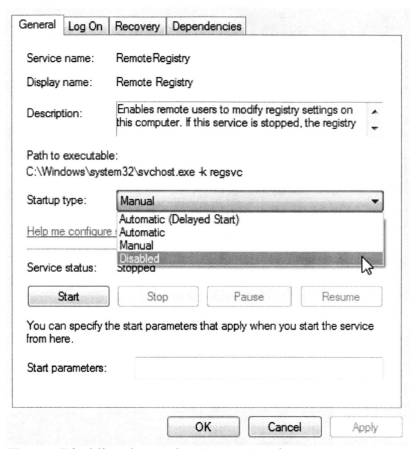

Figure: Disabling the service Remote Registry

If after disabling a service you are experiencing any problems, follow the same instructions above to return the service to the same state as before you disabled it, whether the **Startup type:** was originally *Automatic (Delayed Start)*, *Automatic* or *Manual*.

Chapter 7: Basic Windows Security

Introduction

A very simple, but often overlooked, strategy for protecting your computer is to get in the habit of invoking your screensaver when away from your computer.

In order to best protect your computer, you must also understand the basics of Windows 'User Accounts'. Windows lets you set up different user accounts on a computer so that multiple users can use the same computer but have their own tailored settings and preferences. This is convenient, but more accounts can also mean more potential points of entry for a hacker to access your computer. You should keep the number of accounts on your computer to a minimum, and remove accounts that you no longer need.

Using Your Screensaver as Security

It is important that you invoke your screensaver whenever away from your computer, even if only for a few minutes. This applies equally for both work and personal computing.

This is simple in Windows and is a matter of holding down at the same time the Control-Alt-Delete keys and, from the menu that appears, selecting **Lock**. Alternatively, you can hold down the **Windows logo key** - on some computers it may look like a cloverleaf - and then press the **L key** to invoke the lock immediately. It is important to do this because an unauthorized person only needs a few seconds to either do damage to your computer or gain access to it. Even in such a short time they could, for example, delete or copy data, read or forward emails, or even install a keylogger program without your knowledge.

Top Tip

Locking your computer with the screensaver is a simple tip that you should get in the habit of doing whenever you leave your computer unattended. You just quickly press the **Windows logo key + L** to invoke the lock.

If you are using encryption software (see 'Chapter 13: Encrypting Your Files to Keep them Safe' starting on page 161), this can be particularly handy. After you invoke the lock, no one will be able to access your computer without your passphrase unless they turn off the computer. If this happens, your data will encrypt automatically and be safe when the computer is powered down and rebooted.

This is not the most advanced of techniques, but will protect you from casual or passer-by snoops, especially at the office!

Renaming the Windows Administrator Account

The **administrator account** acts a 'super user' account. A user logged on as an administrator is permitted to change security settings, install software and hardware, access all files on the computer, and can also make changes to other user accounts. As such, the administrator account is a target for hackers.

If you keep and do not change the default settings for the Windows administrator account, you make it that much easier for a hacker to find. By renaming the administrator account, you add a small barrier, and even it may be enough to discourage a novice hacker and convince him to move on to an easier target.

The user account settings in Windows are reached by typing "user accounts" in the Windows Start menu or selecting these menu choices, ***Start*** > ***Control Panel*** > ***User Accounts and Family Safety*** > ***User Accounts***.

Figure: Windows user accounts menu

Select your current administrator account and then select '**Change your account name**'. Enter the new name you want for the administrator account, and that's it. Easy!

You can even set up a decoy, fake or dummy administrator account to replace the renamed one. This is a good idea as if a hacker does infiltrate your computer and sees the customary administrator account is missing, he will know that it has been renamed and will look for it. Setting up the decoy, fake or dummy administrator account is also easy.

Once you have renamed the administer account by following the instructions above, set up a new (the decoy, fake or dummy) administrator account in name but with *limited* privileges (i.e., a Standard user account type).

In the Start menu type "**user accounts**" and then select **Add or remove user accounts**.

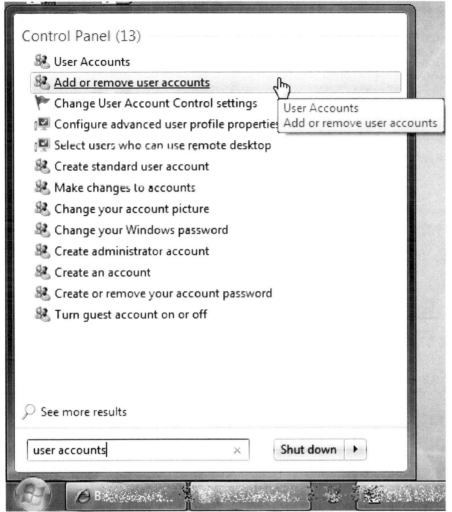

Figure: Accessing user accounts through the Windows start menu

Now select **Create a new account** (shown below).

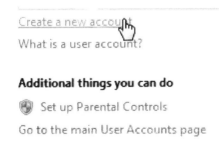

Figure: Creating the decoy administrator user account (part 1)

For the name of the new account, type "Administrator". For account type choose ***Standard user*** (*not* Administrator, because this is the point of setting up the decoy administrator account!) Then click **Create Account**.

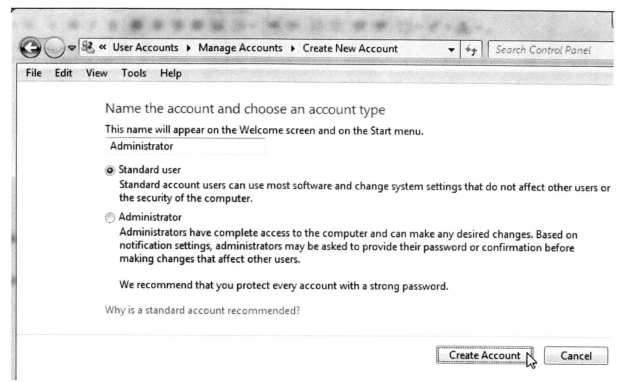

Figure: Creating the decoy administrator user account (part 2)

Now any hacker that pokes around your system and finds what he thinks is the administrator account will be much more limited in the harm he can cause.

Disabling the Windows Guest Account

Because most systems also have a guest account, hackers commonly attempt to hack through it. Disabling the guest account is straight-forward in Windows 7. First, go to the User Accounts menu (see the earlier instructions and screenshots above).

Follow the applicable menu items to get to the guest account and then select **Turn off the guest account** (see the next screenshot).

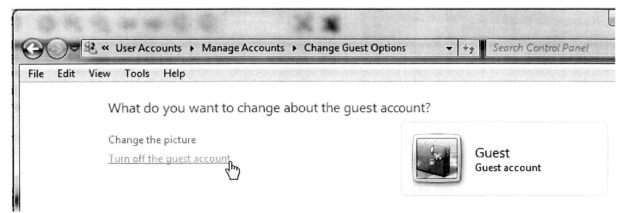

Figure: Disabling the guest account is quick and easy

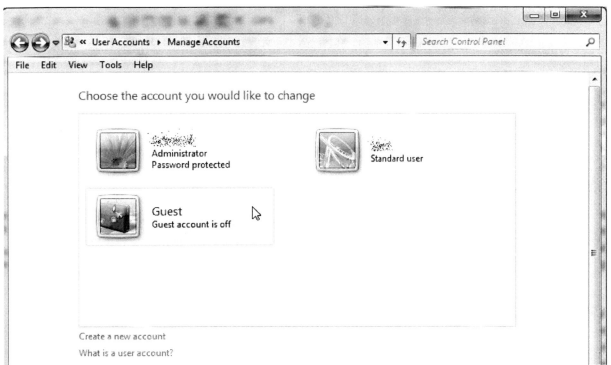

Figure: Confirming that the guest account is now disabled (Guest account is off)

A Special Note for Home Users

Some home users operate in blissful ignorance of these user accounts, and use the Administrator account for all of their tasks by default. They assume that since they are at home (and many times, the only user of the computer), they are safe. They may even use the Administrator account without setting up a password for it.

Do not do this! Think of the scenario where your computer breaks down, and you have to drop it off at the repair shop. The technician now has complete administrative access to your entire computer, your data and programs - a scary thought if your home computer holds financial, medical or other personal information. Similarly, if you are the victim of hackers and they gain access to your computer via this user account, they will have similar unrestricted access.

This bears reiterating - at the very minimum, do the following on your computer, whether at home or at work, and whether you are the sole user of the computer or one of many:

- Protect your user account with a strong passphrase

- Lock your computer using the screensaver

- Rename the Windows Administrator account

- Create a decoy Administrator account

- Disable the Guest account

Chapter 8: Using Firewall Software

Introduction

In the bricks and mortar world, a firewall denotes a protective barrier between you and danger. The term has a similar meaning in the information technology (IT) world. **Firewall software** is software that helps protect your computer from external threats on the Internet. In general terms, firewall software examines incoming data before it reaches your computer to ensure that it is either data you have requested or, if not specifically requested by you, that the data is from a trusted source. It is imperative that you install firewall software on each of your computers.

How to Use Firewall Software

Windows comes with its own personal firewall application. You can access it by clicking on *Start > Control Panel > Security Center*. The steps are illustrated in the figures below.

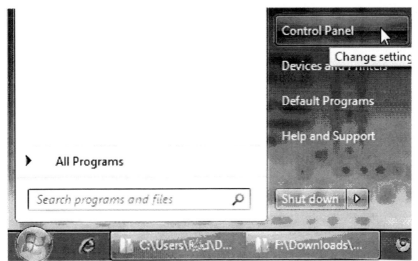

Figure: Selecting the **Control Panel** to access the Windows Firewall

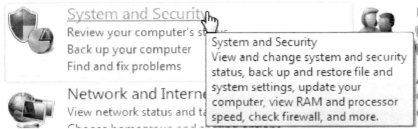

Figure: Then select the **System and Security** settings

Figure: Then select **Windows Firewall**

Figure: Windows Firewall settings

It is also important to know how *exceptions* work. When you install new software applications, they may be blocked from accessing the Internet unless you have added them as an exception to Windows firewall settings. For example, if you engage in online gaming or peer-to-peer (P2P) networking and you do not add the new program to Windows firewall exceptions, the program may not be able to communicate freely through the firewall. Thankfully, often new programs you install ask to be added as exceptions. If not, you may have to add them manually as exceptions.

You may also disable Windows' built-in firewall and use a third-party product instead, some of which are popular and free for personal use. Another advantage of some third-party firewall applications is that they may also watch outbound traffic, not just inbound traffic as with Windows firewall. Monitoring outbound traffic is helpful because it could alert you to any Trojans or spyware initiating outbound communications from your computer to an external destination.

Sometimes a firewall application can be confusing because it prompts you whether to allow certain connections. It is not always obvious which program may be trying to establish a connection.

However, over time you should get the hang of it and the firewall program will eventually "learn" your computer's behavior after you have established which connections to allow or not.

Ports Explained - An Introduction

IP addresses are needed for network communications and are explained in more detail in the 'Introduction to IP Addresses' section on page 121. **Ports** are a similar but different concept altogether. References to ports and port numbers appear in a number of this book's chapters. You can think of ports like radio or television channels. Each port carries a different program you can tune into.

There are 65,536 ports available to your computer for network traffic. Some ports are fixed and reserved for certain types of Internet traffic such as web surfing, sending emails and chatting. The first 1,024 ports (0-1023) have been designated for specific types of Internet traffic. Some of the most familiar ports are listed below.

port 21	-	FTP
port 25	-	SMTP email
port 43	-	WHOIS
port 80	-	HTTP web surfing
port 110	-	POP3 email
port 119	-	NNTP Usenet newsgroups
port 194	-	IRC chat
port 443	-	HTTPS secure, encrypted websites using SSL
port 5010	-	Yahoo! Messenger

Outside the first 1,024 ports, the remainder have not been designated with a specific purpose and are therefore available for other uses, such as for making peer-to-peer (P2P) connections. Ports 1024 to 49151 are registered and not used arbitrarily, but are transient in nature. The upper range, 49152 to 65535 are considered private or dynamic ports. Sometimes, these upper range ports set off alarm bells - in your firewall software for instance - as Trojans, other malware or backdoor programs use them.

If you use a port monitoring utility (see the 'Monitoring Your Ports (Advanced Users)' section on page 142), you will see dozens of ports establishing connections, sitting idle and closed, or listening and waiting for a connection (see the next screenshot).

Figure: A screenshot from CurrPorts, a port monitoring utility

You will also see references to protocols TCP or UDP. **TCP** is a *two-way* type of connection whereas **UDP** is a *one-way* or push broadcasting type of connection. TCP is used to enable two Internet hosts to establish a connection and check that the recipient received all of the data sent from the source. As a result, TCP is more resource intensive than UDP. UDP is often used for more 'quick and dirty' type connections, like media streaming, which do not use robust data verification.

Testing Your Ports

To test your ports from the outside world (i.e., to emulate a hacker's probing to some extent) and assess the effectiveness of your firewall, visit

> http://ww.grc.com/ > Services > ShieldsUp > click on the 'Proceed' button > from the menu select 'Common Ports' (or 'All Service Ports')

> http://www.auditmypc.com/ > Firewall Test

> http://www.pcflank.com/ > Exploits Test

Very cool!

If your firewall is working well, the ports on your computer will appear closed or, even better, non-existent (which is sometimes called "stealth mode"). This means that hackers sniffing and probing around at your ports will not even know you exist - a good thing.

Recommended Firewall Software

At the time of writing, below are some firewall applications that can help protect you against online threats.

ZoneAlarm - freeware
http://www.zonealarm.com/

Deserving its popularity, this free firewall application is easy to use and effective. The software is a little hard to find via the company's link above, so you can also go to http://download.cnet.com/windows/ and search for "zonealarm".

Comodo Internet Security (firewall component) - freeware
http://personalfirewall.comodo.com/

Best known for the quality of its firewall application, Comodo's free package also contains an anti-malware program. You can install each component separately and so do not have to install the anti-virus component if you do not wish. The firewall is simple and flexible making it especially ideal for beginners but offering plenty of features and bells and whistles for advanced users too.

Another Way to Block Undesirable IP Addresses

This is a variant on firewall software that also prevents undesirable IP addresses (e.g., spammers) from connecting to your computer. This type of software should be used *in addition to* your usual firewall software.

PeerBlock (by PeerBlock LLC); freeware
http://www.peerblock.com/

PeerBlock comes with default libraries of undesirable IP addresses and automatically keeps them up-to-date. At the same time, the block lists are also fully user-configurable should you need to tweak the settings and, for whatever reason, permanently or temporarily allow a blocked site. PeerBlock is an effective way to protect your system; kind of like a peer reviewed firewall program.

Chapter 9: Dangers of Wireless Networks and "Hotspots"

Introduction

Wireless networking has become so easy and people so relaxed about it, that this is precisely why it can be a significant threat. You may have noticed when using a laptop computer with a wireless card that you pick up and are even able to connect to all sorts of unsecured networks. This offers up the possibility to use someone else's bandwidth.

Wireless equipment can now operate over a long range and extend to the apartment or house next door and even to the roadside in front of your home. Professional hackers known as "war drivers" are in search of available wireless networks and have special equipment to pick up available signals even from a greater range. Sometimes these attackers post the details of open networks, along with GPS coordinates, and share the information with other hackers.

More About: Wardriving

Widely available software can be used to detect nearby wireless networks and the detection process is sometimes referred to as **wardriving**. Wardriving is where hackers drive around in a car with a portable laptop trying to detect accessible wireless networks in a community. If you don't follow the basic security precautions discussed in this chapter, your wireless network will be open to the public and may be accessible from a surprisingly large distance, including by your neighbors or by hackers parked on the street outside where you live.

You should spend some time reading the instruction manual for your wireless networking hardware equipment. It is important to take the time to understand its features and take steps to secure yourself. Not only could you be hacked, but your connection could literally be taken over and used to launch attacks on other victims from your computer. Hackers could route spam or launch Trojans or distributed denial of service (DDoS) attacks (see the box below) using your connection and equipment. In these cases, it would be your IP address showing up in any computer logs. In other words, the local authorities could be knocking on your door to ask you questions!

! Warning ! Zombie Alert and **Denial of Service Attacks**

Zombies are computers taken over by hackers and used to launch unwitting attacks on other computers.

A **distributed denial of service** attack (or DDoS attack) occurs when an Internet website becomes overloaded under a barrage of web page requests, sometimes being sent from an army of enlisted zombies (as described above). Other users trying to access the same website will be denied access to it due to the burden on the website under attack.

Wireless networking, whether at your home, workplace or public "hotspot," often makes the task of data thieves, hackers and other no-gooders much easier.

In addition to all the usual safeguards and techniques (keeping your operating system and anti-malware software updated), there are some extra precautions you must take if using a wireless network.

Disabling File Sharing

Years ago, this was a much greater threat when file sharing was enabled by default in Windows. Unsuspecting computer users were leaving their systems open to Trojan backdoor attacks. Now, the default setting for newer operating systems, including Windows 7, is to have file-sharing disabled. This is a good thing.

File sharing can be particularly risky over a public network, like your local coffee shop's Internet hotspot service. Depending on your shared settings, you may be exposing your laptop's hard drive to complete strangers.

It only takes a moment to check and confirm your shared file settings are disabled, so do it! Perhaps someone has changed the settings without telling you or you are using an older operating system.

In the Windows start menu, type "advanced shared settings" (shown in the next screenshot).

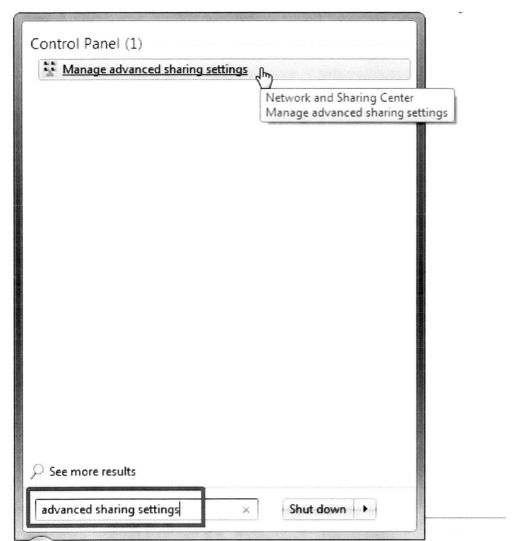

Figure: Going directly to the Control Panel's advanced sharing settings

Or, type "control panel" and then click on the relevant Control Panel items until you reach *Network and Sharing Center > Advanced sharing settings* (see the screenshot below).

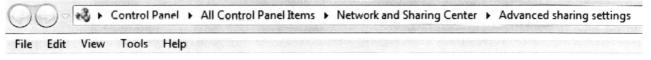

Figure: Where to find Window 7's file sharing settings

From here, you can verify that file sharing is already disabled or, if not, you can disable file sharing (see the next screenshot).

Change sharing options for different network profiles

Windows creates a separate network profile for each network you use. You can choose specific options for each profile.

Home or Work (current profile)

Network discovery

When network discovery is on, this computer can see other network computers and devices and is visible to other network computers. What is network discovery?

- ◉ Turn on network discovery
- ○ Turn off network discovery

File and printer sharing

When file and printer sharing is on, files and printers that you have shared from this computer can be accessed by people on the network.

- ○ Turn on file and printer sharing
- ◉ Turn off file and printer sharing

Figure: Making sure that file sharing is turned off, as above

Properly Configuring Your Router

If you have high-speed Internet access at home or at your business, you likely have a **router** (usually a box with blinking lights on it). This is a box that lets multiple computers use the same high-speed connection to access the Internet. Wireless routers are very popular nowadays, allowing computers within a specified range to use the services of the router without the need to have messy wires running from each computer to the router box.

There are a few key things to keep in mind with routers. Although these tips are simple, many people do not apply them and are open to online attacks and threats.

Changing the Default Username and Passphrase

The first thing you should always do, right from the start, is change the router's default password. For example, most home wireless routers now come with a web interface with the default username "admin" and the password "admin". If left unchanged, it's easy for hackers to use these default username and passwords.

It is important that you change these default values. Otherwise, even an amateur hacker could gain access to your wireless router. Default passwords are easy for hackers to determine since they are widely available online or in user manuals (also online). As always, use a strong passphrase.

Disabling Service Set Identifier (SSID) Number Broadcasting

It is also important that you change the service set identifier or **SSID** number for the wireless router. This will help ensure that your wireless network is not being announced to the world at large. A wireless router automatically gives off a signal on a regular basis, broadcasting its ID number. You can easily set up your equipment so that it does not broadcast its SSID number automatically. Rather, better that you manually enter the SSID number into each client piece of equipment (e.g., your desktops and laptops) so that hackers cannot pick the SSID out of the air. If SSID broadcasting is turned-off, hackers of the wardriving variety will not even be aware of you.

Please check the manufacturer's manual on how to turn off your specific wireless equipment's SSID broadcasting. It is usually a matter of finding the correct option in the menu and simply disabling it. Easy!

Encrypting Your Wireless Connection

Technology is changing all the time and wireless Internet routers are no exception. At the same time, the routers are backward compatible meaning that they will still support older technologies. This can be especially important for the encryption method you use for your router.

Without getting into the entire mumbo jumbo make sure your router is configured to use the latest encryption method which is **WPA** or **WPA2**. The older technology, WEP, is now easily cracked using widely available software utilities. So double-check to make sure that your router is configured to use WPA/WPA2.

Using Media Access Codes (MACs)

Another excellent source of protection is to restrict your wireless network on the basis of media access codes (**MAC**). Each wireless device has its own MAC address. So, you can set up your wireless network to only work with the MAC numbers you permit.

This means that you can set up your router to only be accessible by machines with the MAC addresses that you specify. By doing this, the router's presence will go undetected by other equipment whose MAC numbers have *not* been entered in the router's setup. The process varies from device to device, so check your router's manual for details.

More About: MAC

A media access code (**MAC**) is like a social security number that uniquely identifies a piece of computer equipment.

With this technique, when you buy or otherwise introduce new devices (e.g., a new laptop) to your network you will need to enter the new device's MAC address into the settings for your network through the router software.

Using this technique will help ensure that unknown devices are not accessing your wireless network.

How to Determine Your MAC

By way of example, to determine the MAC address for your computer's wireless network card, type **command** in the Start menu, and select **Command Prompt** (as shown in the screenshots that follow).

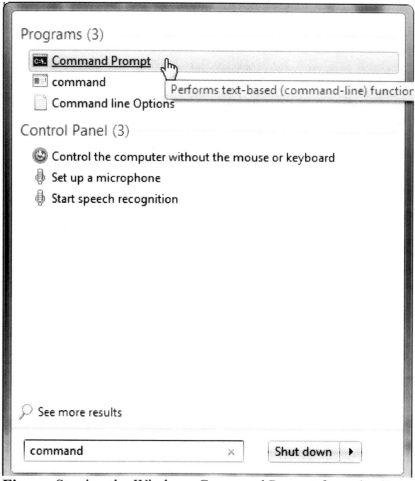

Figure: Starting the Windows Command Prompt from the Start menu

A DOS-like window will open. If you type **IPCONFIG /ALL** a list (usually not too long) of your devices and configurations will be displayed. Look for your **Wireless Network Adapter** (if you connect wirelessly) or Ethernet adapter **Local Area Connection** (if you connect with a cable), and note the long series of letters, numbers and dashes beside **Physical Address**.

Voila! You have now determined the MAC address (00-13-CE-3C-39-BA in the screenshot below).

```
Microsoft Windows [Version 6.1.7600]
Copyright (c) 2009 Microsoft Corporation.  All rights reserved.

C:\Users\Rod>ipconfig /all

Windows IP Configuration

   Host Name . . . . . . . . . . . . : AcerLaptop
   Primary Dns Suffix  . . . . . . . :
   Node Type . . . . . . . . . . . . : Hybrid
   IP Routing Enabled. . . . . . . . : No
   WINS Proxy Enabled. . . . . . . . : No
   DNS Suffix Search List. . . . . . : kabsi.at

Wireless LAN adapter Wireless Network Connection:

   Connection-specific DNS Suffix  . : kabsi.at
   Description . . . . . . . . . . . : Intel(R) PRO/Wireless 2200BG Network Conn
ection
   Physical Address. . . . . . . . . : 00-13-CE-3C-39-BA
   DHCP Enabled. . . . . . . . . . . : Yes
   Autoconfiguration Enabled . . . . : Yes
   Link-local IPv6 Address . . . . . : fe80::f9a8:69c7:9005:9edc%14(Preferred)
   IPv4 Address. . . . . . . . . . . : 192.168.1.101(Preferred)
   Subnet Mask . . . . . . . . . . . : 255.255.255.0
   Lease Obtained. . . . . . . . . . : 11 July 2010 10:49:00
   Lease Expires . . . . . . . . . . : 12 July 2010 10:49:00
   Default Gateway . . . . . . . . . : 192.168.1.1
   DHCP Server . . . . . . . . . . . : 192.168.1.1
   DHCPv6 IAID . . . . . . . . . . . : 369103822
   DHCPv6 Client DUID. . . . . . . . : 00-01-00-01-12-90-E5-17-00-C0-9F-E4-B2-5C

   DNS Servers . . . . . . . . . . . : 195.202.128.2
                                       195.202.128.3
   NetBIOS over Tcpip. . . . . . . . : Enabled
```

Figure: Displaying the MAC address of your adapters with the IPCONFIG /ALL command

Once you have the information you need, exit the command window by typing **Exit**. You will now need to enter the relevant MAC address in your router's settings.

Changing the (Subnet) IP Address

You should also change the internal IP subnet - the range of IP addresses allowed within your router's network - if possible. Most hackers know that the default subnet for home routers is 192.168.0 and that the administrative access can be gained at http://192.168.0.1/. You can use any number from zero to 254 (i.e., 192.168.xxx) where the third subset of numbers xxx can be anywhere from zero to 254), but you will not need the entire range unless you have a lot of equipment. Most people simply pick zero (192.168.0) and so you should choose something else. Using a number further along the range will mean that any potential attackers must work that much harder, hopefully give up and move on to easier targets.

Using Hotspots Securely

"Hotspots" or public wireless networks are more and more popular and showing up in all sorts of cafés, airports, restaurants and bars. While offering convenience, you must appreciate that you are sharing an unknown network with an unknown number of unknown people.

Of course, you should already be honoring the most basic elements of security described elsewhere in this book: making sure that your anti-malware software is up-to-date, using personal firewall software, and protecting your most sensitive and critical accounts with strong passphrases. Better yet, hopefully your sensitive data is locked away using encryption (discussed in an upcoming chapter).

Beware of Spoofers and Phishers

Although it sounds obvious, you should also make sure that you are connected to the actual hotspot (!) rather than a decoy, fake or "spoofed" site. For example, there is software that allows a hacker sitting nearby to make you believe that you are logging on to the hotspot when, in fact, you are entering your username and passphrase into a fake portal and thereby giving them to the hacker. The spoofing software allows a hacker to create a replica of the hotspot's login page and fool you (phish you) into providing the username and passphrase and sometimes even credit card numbers.

To make sure that you are on the correct sign-in page look carefully at the URL in your browser bar. In addition, most sign-in pages are through a secure connection so look for the https at the start of the URL (as shown below).

Figure: Internet Explorer displays the https and a lock icon when a secure connection is made

Beware of Sniffers

There are other hacker software programs called sniffers which can capture your data zipping around the airwaves (i.e., your passphrases, emails and credit card information). As above, use only verified https connections as this means that the data you send from your computer is being encrypted enroute, so if it is intercepted the information will be completely unintelligible to the hackers.

To protect yourself, trust your instincts and always have a look around to make sure that you do not have any overly curious neighbor sitting close to you. That said, these hackers do not even have to be sitting near you and could even be sitting in a car parked across the street.

PART II - SAFEGUARDING YOUR COMPUTER AND BEING SAFE ONLINE

In this part, you will learn more advanced techniques to increase your security, protect your privacy and maximize your online anonymity.

→ Chapter 10: Covering Your Tracks and Washing Up

→ Chapter 11: Protecting Your Identity and IP Address with Anonymous Surfing

→ Chapter 12: Getting Downloads Using Torrents and Peer-to-Peer (P2P)

→ Chapter 13: Encrypting Your Files to Keep them Safe

→ Chapter 14: Wiping Your Sensitive Data

→ Chapter 15: Using Email, Webmail and Remailers

→ Chapter 16: Usenet Newsgroups

→ Chapter 17: Chat, IRC and Instant Messaging

Chapter 10: Covering Your Tracks and Washing Up

Introduction

People entrust their most private information to their computer, including financial and business records, travel plans, love letters, and health information. Sometimes you might not even realize you're storing sensitive information on your computer. You might briefly visit a website for health advice, but your browser could automatically leave a long-lasting record of that visit on your computer. Anyone with access to the computer could find out what health issues you have been researching.

You might be surprised how easy it is to uncover information like this, even after you've deleted it. This chapter starts by highlighting the extent to which information is left behind on your computer, especially after being on the Internet. You'll learn how to cover your web surfing tracks and keep your activities private. You'll learn about forensic software that can be used to reveal hidden information on your computer, and about the tools you can use to combat it and ensure your data is irrecoverable.

This chapter concludes by looking at how you can clean sensitive information from the guts of your operating system (your Registry and some other special Windows files).

Why You Need to Remove Trace Data from Your Computer

Once information is accessed or stored on your computer, that information could be recovered even after being deleted (and emptied from the Recycle Bin). Hard drive capacities are now so large that data and information from many years ago (including deleted files) could still be recovered in perfect condition.

Imagine what somebody would learn about you if they looked at the sites you visited on the Internet, your most recently used documents, and files you've deleted from the hard drive. By digging a bit deeper, they could discover data that is even harder to get rid of on your computer such as the filenames of documents, pictures, video clips or web pages that you searched for, downloaded, saved, opened, renamed or deleted.

These risks are particularly important if you ever sell or dispose of your computer or its storage media, whether hard drives or removable USB sticks. If you do not properly go about removing the data, it could be easily recovered and used by identity thieves.

There are a number of things you can do to ensure that information like this cannot be recovered so "wash up" and protect your privacy. Some techniques can be accomplished manually, but software is a big help, as you'll see.

Top Tip

Throughout this book, "washing up" and to "wash" or "wash up" refer to the process of cleansing personal data from your computer. "Washing software" means the software you can use to do this.

Records your Web Browser Keeps

Web browsers record every site you visit, every link you follow, every image you view, and also keep a record of your downloads and favorite websites. Much of this information is found in the browser's **history**, **cookies** and **cache**.

The **history** is simply a list of websites that you visited in the past x days, depending on the options and preferences set in your browser. To see your browser history in Internet Explorer 9, select the 'favorites center' icon (the star, as shown below) or Favorites on the menu bar, and then select the History tab.

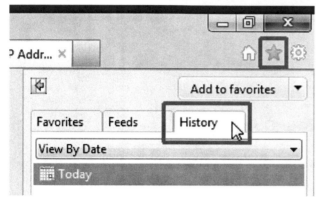

Figure: The screenshot above illustrates how to access the *History* in Internet Explorer 9

To see your browser history in Internet Explorer 8 for example, select from the menu, ***View > Explorer Bars > History*** (shown in the next screenshot).

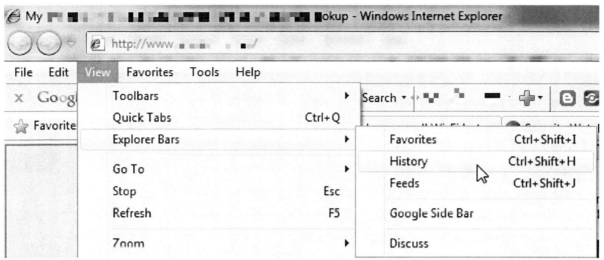

Figure: The screenshot above illustrates how to access the *History* in Internet Explorer 8

Cookies are small text files downloaded to your computer from a website to help it to identify you. Cookies enable websites to remember your user preferences and settings, track your navigation of the site, offer you extra services or even log on to the site automatically. For example, eBay offers to keep you logged in, so you only have to enter your password once per day. When you come back again, eBay uses the cookie it put on your computer to recognize you and lets you in without asking you to enter your password again. Another example is Amazon.com which uses cookies to know when you return to its website and, in combination with its back-end databases, remind you about your past searches and display recommendations for additional products.

Depending on your browser settings, cookies may be stored on your computer without your knowledge. Most websites use cookies and some use more than one.

While cookies do help personalize your settings for a site, they also have their drawbacks. For example, because a cookie uniquely identifies your browser from your **IP address**, the website can build a profile about you and, perhaps, provide this information to other parties, including advertisers. Some advertising networks use cookies to track the adverts you view across different websites you visit too.

Note that just the existence of a cookie on your computer could be a privacy risk because it contains the website's name. For example, if you visit websites about finding a new job or self-diagnosing a health complaint, somebody could find out by looking at the cookies on your computer.

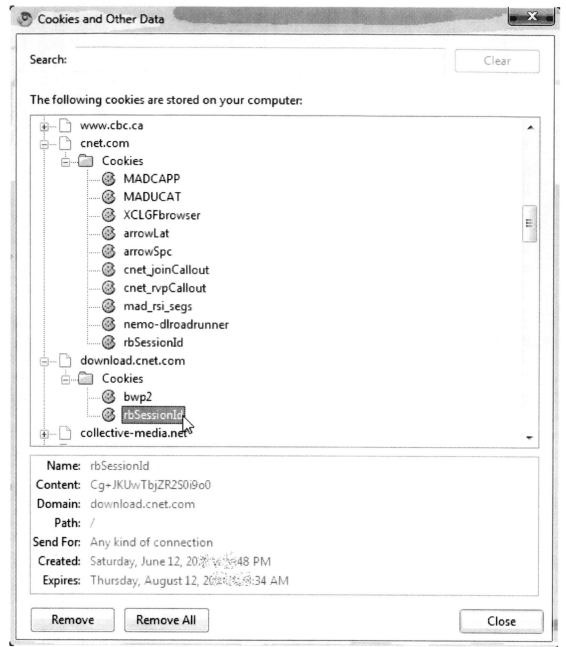

Figure: Cookie information as displayed in the Chrome browser

From the figure above, you can see that the user has visited the websites www.cbc.ca, cnet.com, download.cnet.com and collective-media.net. In Chrome, this information is freely accessible from the following menu choices: Customize and control (the *wrench icon*) > *Options* > *Under the Hood* > *Content Settings… * > *Cookies* > *Show cookies and other site data*.

> **More About: Cookies**
> A **cookie** has at least two elements: a name and a value. The **name** is just the name for the piece of data in the following value. The **value** can contain any number of things; it usually contains the relevant domain name of the server that delivered the cookie, an expiration date of the cookie, and applicable user data like usernames and passphrases (hopefully encrypted but not always!)

While your browser history records your recent website visits, your browser **cache** saves the *actual* web pages you have viewed. The cache uses these copies of web pages to make your browsing experience faster when you revisit a website. Instead of downloading the same file twice, the browser will take it from the cache if it's there. Clearly, the contents of the cache represent a risk to your privacy because they show the web pages and images you've viewed online. Even when you empty your cache, the information may still be stored in the cache's index file.

Similarly, website addresses (URLs) you save as **favorites** or **bookmarks** in your browser are easily located and reveal your preferred websites.

Removing the Records Your Browser Keeps

As seen above, most web browsers keep extensive records of your online activity.

At a minimum, you should delete your entire browsing history after visiting any sensitive websites. Better yet, most browsers now allow you to enter a kind of 'stealth mode' to disable the browser's history and tracking features before you start visiting websites. Instructions and screenshots follow for Internet Explorer, Firefox and Chrome.

If you have an older or different browser not illustrated below, use your favorite search engine to find the necessary instructions.

Internet Explorer

Deleting your tracks in Internet Explorer is now much easier than in the past. From the menu, choose the ***Tools icon > Safety > Delete browsing history…***

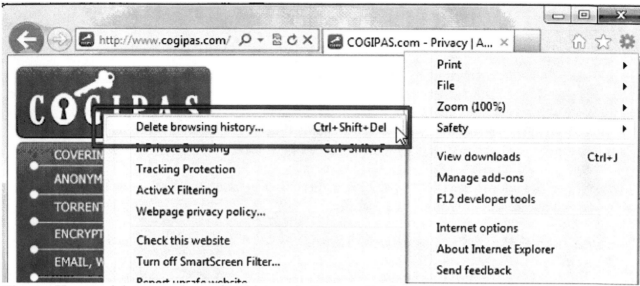

Figure: How to delete your browsing history in Internet Explorer 9

Now choose the various sub-options you want to clear and click **Delete** (shown in the next screenshot).

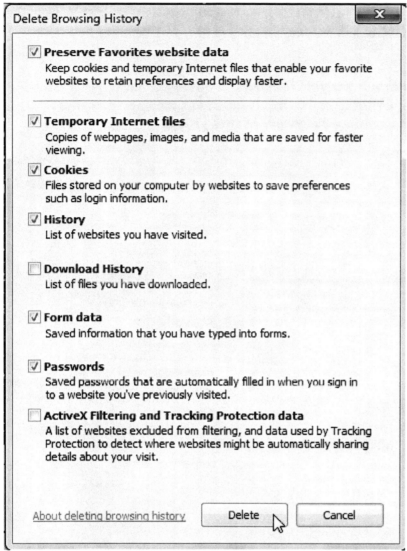

Figure: Select the records you want to clear and click Delete

IE's Stealth Mode

You can also disable Internet Explorer's record-keeping features *before* you visit any sensitive websites.

From the same menu select the ***Tools icon > Safety > InPrivate Browsing***. Your browser's screen will change to indicate that you are now surfing in the 'InPrivate' mode, meaning that your browser has stopped caching files and recording the history of sites visited.

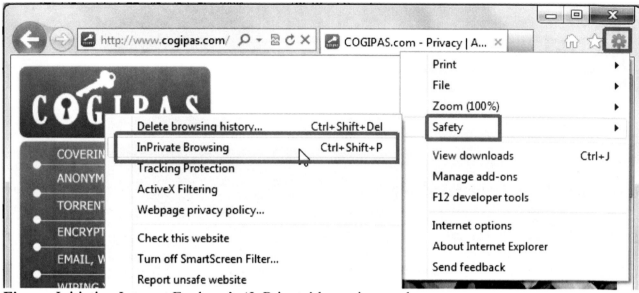

Figure: Initiating Internet Explorer's 'InPrivate' browsing mode

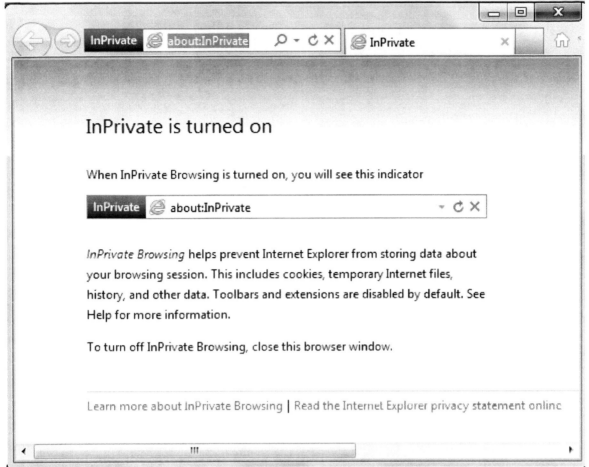

Figure: Internet Explorer's InPrivate browsing mode is now activated

Mozilla Firefox

To clear your history in Firefox, go to the menu and select ***Tools > Clear Recent History*** (shown in the next screenshot).

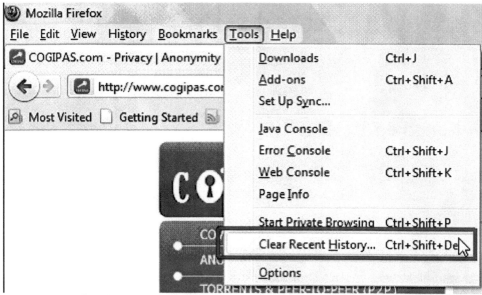

Figure: Navigating to Firefox's Clear Recent History feature. (If you cannot see the menu bar choices in Firefox, select the orange Firefox box in the upper-right corner > ***Options*** > ***Menu Bar***)

You will be presented with a Clear Recent History box. Click on the ***Details*** options and also select the ***Time range*** that you wish to clear.

Once you are happy with your settings, click on ***Clear Now***.

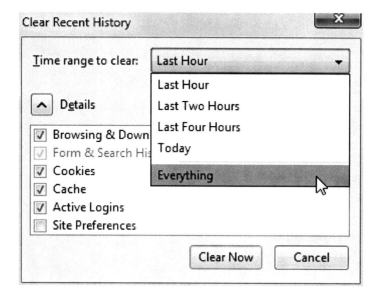

Your browsing history will then be deleted according to the options you selected.

You can also set up Firefox so that it does not record your activities in the first place. From Firefox's menu, select ***Tools > Options > Privacy tab*** (which looks like an opera mask).

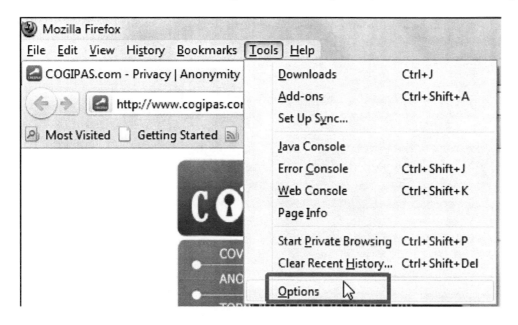

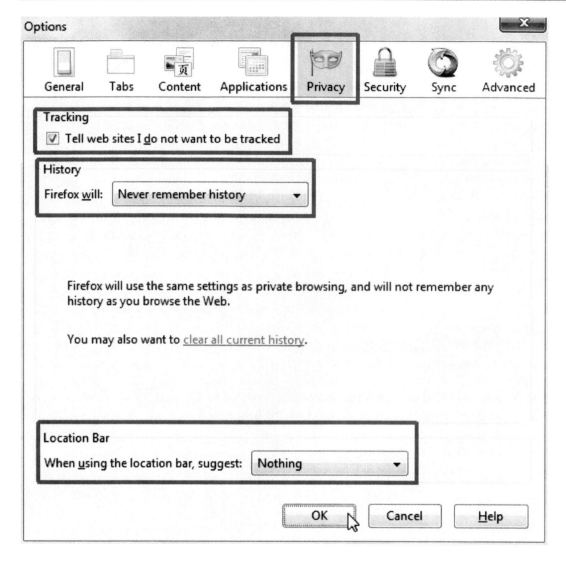

Now change the **Tracking**, **History** and **Location Bar** settings, as illustrated above. The latest version of Firefox enables you to prevent websites from tracking you. Select the checkbox *Tell web sites I do not want to be tracked*. The Location bar suggests sites for you on the basis of your previously visited sites and can sometimes display suggested sites that you rather wish it hadn't.

Next move to the **Advanced tab** within Options, click **Network** and clear your **Offline Storage** (which is the cache of web pages you've visited) – shown in the next screenshot.

Figure: Clearing Firefox's cache of stored files on your computer

Firefox's Stealth Mode

To use Firefox in
stealth mode, go to
the menu and select
***Tools > Start Private
Browsing***.

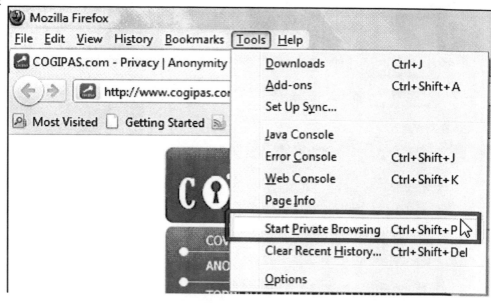

You might receive a short warning message in a dialogue box (especially the first time you launch Private Browsing). Once you select Start Private Browsing, you will be presented with the new Private Browsing screen confirming that Firefox will not record the history of your session.

 Private Browsing

Firefox won't remember any history for this session.

In a Private Browsing session, Firefox won't keep any browser history, search history, download history, web form history, cookies, or temporary internet files. However, files you download and bookmarks you make will be kept.

To stop Private Browsing, select Tools > Stop Private Browsing, or close Firefox.

ⓘ While this computer won't have a record of your browsing history, your internet service provider or employer can still track the pages you visit.

Learn More

Figure: Firefox's Private Browsing mode is now enabled

If you want to go back to normal browsing mode, select ***Tools > Stop Private Browsing***, as illustrated below.

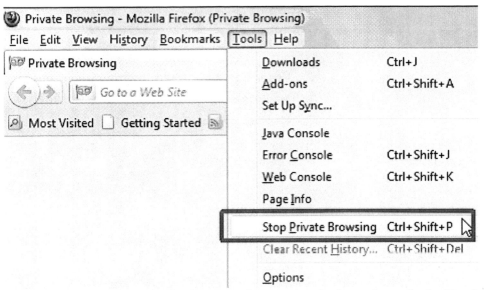

Figure: Re-enabling Firefox's normal browsing is done through the Tools menu item

Google Chrome

To delete your tracks in Chrome, go to the menu and choose the Customize and Control icon (the wrench icon). Then click **Tools** > **Clear browsing data** (see the next screenshot).

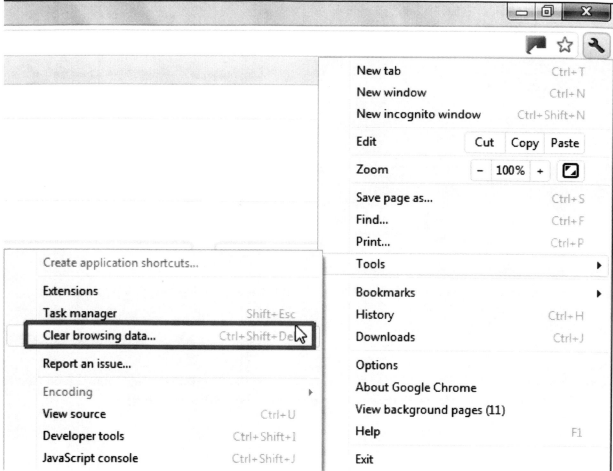

Figure: Clearing browser data in Firefox

You will be presented with a *Clear Browsing Data* box. Select the items and the period of time that you wish to cover.

Once you are happy with your settings, click *Clear Browsing Data*.

Your browsing records are now deleted according to the options you selected.

Chrome's Stealth Mode

To use Chrome in its stealth mode (called incognito), click the Customize and Control icon (the wrench icon) and then select *New incognito window*.

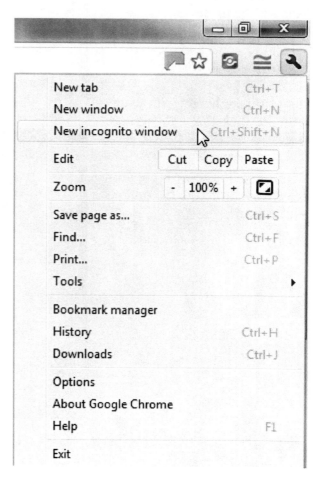

You will be presented with a new incognito browsing screen confirming that no records of your session will be recorded by Chrome (shown in the next screenshot).

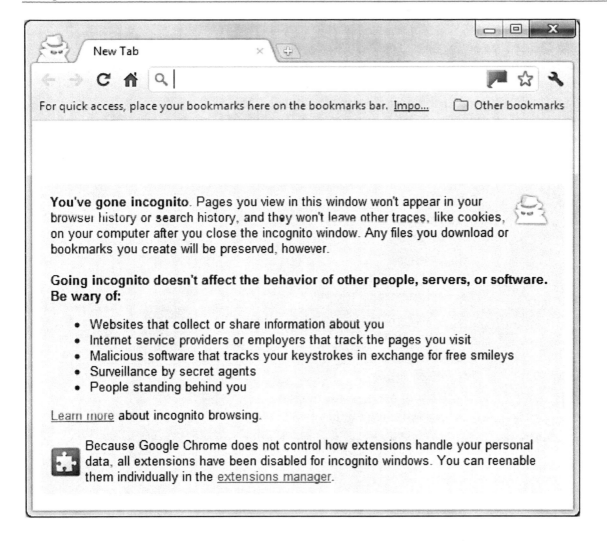

Congratulations, you have taken the basic steps to making sure that your browser tracks are now cleared.

A Caveat to Keep in Mind (Advanced Users)

However, do not forget that even if you delete your browser records, somebody might be able to recover them including with forensic software. Internet Explorer, for example, uses a file called INDEX.DAT which acts as a database of history and cookies and other browser traces. Like any other data, the deleted contents of INDEX.DAT could be recovered.

For added protection, use a browser installed to an *encrypted drive* (see 'Chapter 13: Encrypting Your Files to Keep them Safe' starting on page 161). For ever more complete protection, after you delete your browser records, *purge* the old file and folder names from your system and wipe the free space on your computer's hard drive (see 'Chapter 14: Wiping Your Sensitive Data' starting on page 173).

Clearing Your Most Recently Used (MRU) Records

Depending on your settings, Windows keeps a list of the most recently used (MRU) items you have accessed on your computer, including documents, images, and videos. It also stores the most recent Searches performed and Run commands executed. These MRU records are easily accessible from the Windows Start button under the fly-out menu item Recent Items.

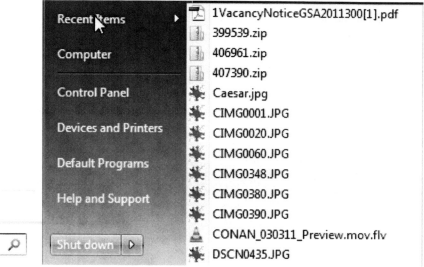

Figure: Window's Recent Items, accessible from the Start button, are an example of a MRU record

Windows MRU records are easy to disable: in the Start box type 'Taskbar' and you should see the 'Taskbar and Start Menu' Control Panel item displayed in the menu (see the next screenshot). Select it and **uncheck** the 'Privacy' selections, as shown on page 94.

Figure: Finding and opening the 'Taskbar and Start Menu' Control Panel item

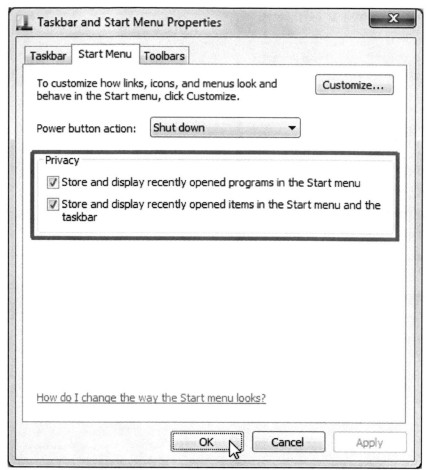

Figure: Disabling Windows most recently used settings: *un*check the items shown above

In addition, many individual software applications also have their own MRU features. Although they are meant to save you time when searching for recently used items, they enable anyone with access to your computer to open your programs and quickly see what files you have been accessing with them.

If the file or download is still in the same place on your computer (it hasn't been moved, encrypted, renamed or saved onto a removable drive or USB stick), selecting the item in the list of MRU records will actually open it. You should check the Preferences, Setup or Options for each application to see if it is possible to disable its MRU features. An example is shown below.

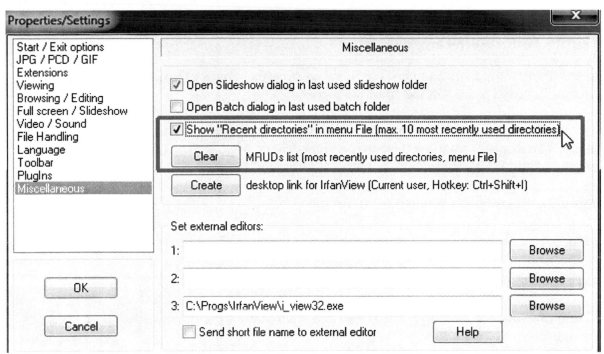

Figure: To disable the MRU feature and clear the existing MRU records in the popular image viewer IrfanView, you go into the Miscellaneous Settings

The Records Your Registry Keeps

As discussed above, Windows and most applications store the names of your most recently used (MRU) items. But MRUs are just the tip of the iceberg.

Windows consolidates and centralizes many settings and configurations into a complex database, the **Registry**. The Registry tracks and records a great deal of what is done on your computer. Therefore, it can also be a gold mine of sensitive information for snoops and identity thieves.

For example, the Registry can be analyzed to reveal:

- records of websites and URLs you have visited (separate from your web browser's history),

- the names of downloaded files,

- where downloaded files originated from and where they were downloaded to on your computer,

- passphrases stored by applications for the websites and services you use (although well designed applications *should* store passphrases securely in encrypted from),

- lists of connected and previously mounted storage devices,

- the names of Usenet newsgroups you subscribe to,

- records of wireless networks that the computer logged into,

- and more!

You can see how some of this information could come back to haunt you. To make matters worse, some forensic computer software packages quickly analyze and extract information from the Registry in just a few clicks.

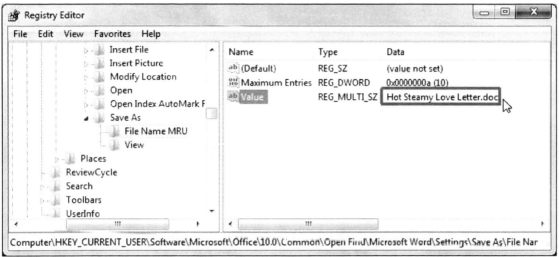

Figure: Oops. Sometimes the Registry can reveal information that you rather it didn't

Because the potentially sensitive information mentioned above is tucked away in the Registry, it can be difficult to find and purge. While you can pick through your information by manually browsing through your Registry (see the next section) it is better to use software to take care of this for you, sometimes even automatically. See the 'Recommended Software for Clearing Unwanted Trace Data' on page 116.

Cleaning Your Registry of Trace Data (Advanced Users)

Introduction

Many of the methods outlined in this book will protect you from privacy breaches. However, one tricky problem is how to remove the filenames, folder paths, search terms, and website histories that get embedded in your Registry. Even though your files may be safeguarded by encryption, somebody could discover a sensitive filename in your Registry, which reveals significant information about you.

In this section, you will learn how to clean data from your Registry. The Registry also contains information that Windows requires to work correctly, so take particular care when accessing it.

Accessing the Registry

> **! Warning !**
> When using **Regedit**, be careful only to *view* entries and not to delete or change any entries because this could cause serious problems in Windows, including stopping your computer from booting up.

Part 1: Finding the Sensitive Information

Click on the Windows Start button and type in "regedit", as shown below. When you see *regedit.exe*, click on it.

Figure: Starting the Registry Editor

Figure: Registry Editor's interface is a bit like that of Windows Explorer, which is used for browsing files on your hard drive. They both show roots and branches

Once Registry Editor opens, go to Registry Editor's menu and choose *Edit > Find* (or press **Ctrl + F**).

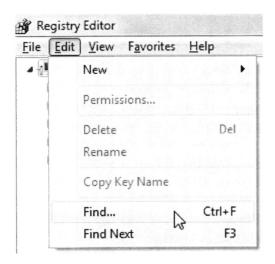

Type your search term in the dialogue box and click **OK**. In the example below, "\downloads\" is used, but you can enter whatever term you like that relates to the sensitive activities you wish to keep private. You can repeat the same search throughout your Registry by pressing **F3** (or choosing from the menu *Edit > Find Again*). Keep going until you are told that you have reached the end of the Registry. The searches are *not* case sensitive.

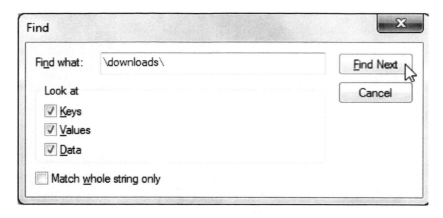

Good strings to search for are:

- File and folder names related to your sensitive online activities

- Some other terms that reflect your sensitive online activities (e.g., terms that relate to health issues you recently searched)

- the downloads folder path (e.g., "\downloads\" without quotes)

- "Recent", "history", "log", "MRU" (short for 'most recently used') without quotes or other specific terms that may reveal your sensitive activities

- File extensions related to your sensitive activities (you will turn up lots of innocuous hits, but this is a thorough method)

  o documents and texts (e.g., .DOC, .PDF or .TXT files)
  o videos, movies and films (e.g., .MPG, .AVI, .WMV files)
  o pictures and images (e.g., .JPG, .PNG files)
  o BitTorrents (e.g., .TORRENT files)
  o sounds and tones (e.g., .MP3, .WAV files)

- The drive letter of your encrypted drive (see 'Chapter 13: Encrypting Your Files to Keep them Safe')

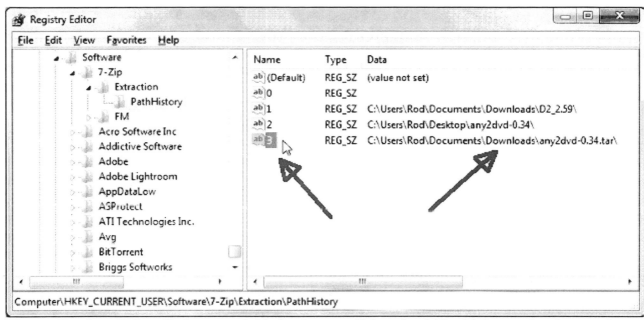

Figure: Registry Editor finds a search hit for the term "\downloads\" which reveals what you have been downloading to your computer

Part 2: Removing Sensitive Information from the Registry

As you find sensitive information in your Registry, add its location to Registry Editor's Favorites for your future reference and the next steps described below. To do this, go to the menu and choose *Favorites > Add to Favorites*.

You can later use this Registry information to clean the Registry by:

- Clearing the entries manually. You can delete entries manually (be careful!) by clearing out the actual *Value data.* To do this, double-click on the entry that your search has just highlighted. A small window will open showing you the Value name: and Value data: of the registry entry that you just double-clicked on.

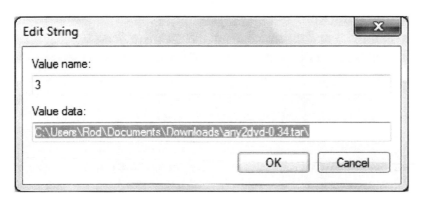

Highlight the sensitive information you wish to delete in the Value data: box, whether some or all of the entry, and simply press delete on your keyboard (or right-click and select Delete) and then click on OK. This instance of the data is now removed from your Registry. You will have to perform similar manual deletes for all of the sensitive hits that you turn up.

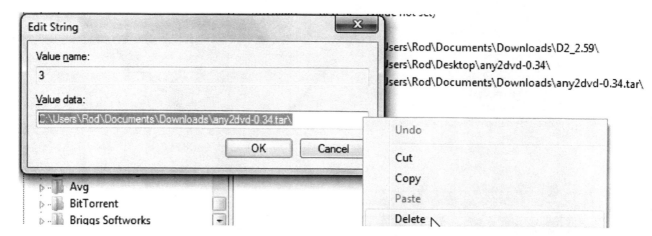

Of course, this can be a major hassle because you would have to do this every time you engage in sensitive activities. This would be in addition to taking other prudent steps that you will learn about later in this book such as wiping your *hard drive's free space* and *purging empty directory entries* (see 'Chapter 14: Wiping Your Sensitive Data' starting on page 173).

- <u>Creating a Registry batch file</u>. It is possible to create a Registry **batch file** (*.REG or *.INF) that can flush out these sensitive key entries when you double-click it. However, given the number of good software utilities that can do this job, it is recommended that you keep life simple and use washing software instead.

- <u>Adding a custom item for removal to your washing software</u> (see the list of suitable software products at page 116). This is the easiest approach, and is the recommended one. Most good washing software lets you add custom Registry entries to its list of items to wash. Even if you use washing software you may wish to manually search the Registry to find the locations of sensitive data in the first place and to confirm that the washing software is doing its job properly and purging the sensitive data from your system.

Other Tips

You can also:

- If available, turn off your programs' MRU features. These are usually found under the menu items 'Options', 'Preferences' or 'Settings'.

- Use programs that do not use most recently used (MRU) features. To identify them, there is little choice but to carefully read each program's documentation or to consult community software forums.

- Install the programs that you use for sensitive activities on an encrypted virtual drive or, better yet, set up an encrypted or even hidden operating system as this will safeguard the Registry behind a wall of strong encryption (see 'Chapter 13: Encrypting Your Files to Keep them Safe' starting on page 161).

Cleaning Difficult Trace Data from Your System

Log files, metadata and temporary files created by your software can remain on your computer too, sometimes for years. It's even possible to recover information from your computer's memory (RAM) for a short period of time after you have shutdown your computer. So, in addition to worrying about protecting the privacy and security of the *content* you actually create or download yourself, you also have to worry about what your software is storing on your computer in the background and out of plain sight.

Removing Temporary Files

Windows and a number of applications use the C:\WINDOWS\TEMP\ folder to save data temporarily. If a process is interrupted, an application quits unexpectedly or the application does not bother cleaning up its efforts afterwards, data may be left behind in this folder.

You can dig around in your own C:\WINDOWS\TEMP\ folder to see what gems lie in wait.

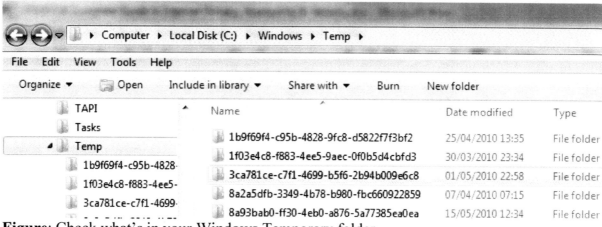

Figure: Check what's in your Windows Temporary folder

You can usually manually delete these temporary contents, or most of them, but any good **washing software** will also take care of this automatically (see the 'Recommended Software for Clearing Unwanted Trace Data' on page 116).

Flushing Cached DNS Entries

Every website has its own IP address, which is its location on the Internet. Domain names are used as a handy way to point the browser at the right IP address, because they are more memorable. When you visit websites, your operating system fetches the underlying IP address through something called a domain name system (or DNS) server. This action is *independent* from your web browser and so **cached DNS entries** will remain in your system even if you run your browser's privacy clean-up features (such as deleting the history, cookies, and cache). In addition, the cached DNS entries will remain in your system even if you visited the websites in a **stealth** browsing session such as Internet Explorer's InPrivate mode, Firefox's Private Browsing mode or Chrome's incognito mode.

You can verify this yourself by typing **command** in the Windows start menu and clicking on the CMD.EXE program to open a command prompt window (also called a DOS prompt). This is shown in the next screenshot.

Figure: Start the Windows command prompt

In the now open command prompt window, type in IFCONFIG /DISPLAYDNS (as shown below). A list of cached DNS entries and the corresponding domain names will be displayed. This further illustrates how easily your privacy could be breached.

Figure: Listing the cached DNS entries on your system with the IPCONFIG /DISPLAYDNS command

You can manually 'flush' (delete) these cached DNS entries in the same command prompt window by typing in IPCONFIG /FLUSHDNS. This is shown in the next screenshot.

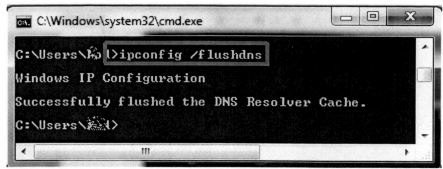

Figure: Running the IPCONFIG /FLUSHDNS command deletes the cached DNS entries

To double-check, run the IPCONFIG /DISPLAYDNS command again to confirm that the cached DNS entries are now gone.

Any good washing software should rid your system of cached DNS entries and save you from this manual step. But you can also use these techniques to verify that your washing software is getting rid of cached DNS entries.

Washing up after Leaky Applications, Compound Files and Private File Systems

Your computer does many things in the background. Some programs 'leak' data or leave lots of information behind in the form of metadata, autosave remnants or other file data which are sometimes referred to as system artifacts. Other applications may keep recoverable copies of potentially sensitive data inside their own proprietary file systems or in file objects. Some applications also store most recently used files and other potentially sensitive information in their own configuration files (*.INI) while others store them in the **Registry**.

Even if your sensitive files, downloads or documents and related software are saved in an encrypted location, one of your software applications may, unknown to you, 'spill' or 'leak' some data to a non-encrypted location where it can be detected.

Top Tip

This 'spilling' or 'leaking' is a big enough problem that separate software exists to address it. For example, see the www.sandboxie.com website for a detailed description of the problem and their solution for it.

Clearing the Windows Paging (Swap) File

When your memory (RAM) becomes full or Windows assigns a computing activity a low priority, Windows writes some data to your hard drive and uses it as so-called *virtual memory*. This virtual memory is stored in a specially designated and protected file, often large, which is usually located at C:\PAGEFILE.SYS (or in older versions of Windows at C:\WINDOWS\WIN386.SWP). This file is called the **paging file**, or sometimes the swap file, because Windows temporarily summons and trades drive space for virtual memory in lieu of RAM.

To see the virtual memory settings in Windows, type "view advanced system settings" in the Start bar. When the system properties menu opens, select the 'Performance Settings' button, then the 'Advanced' tab and then, under the heading 'Virtual memory', press the 'Change…' button.

The virtual memory settings are shown in the next screenshot.

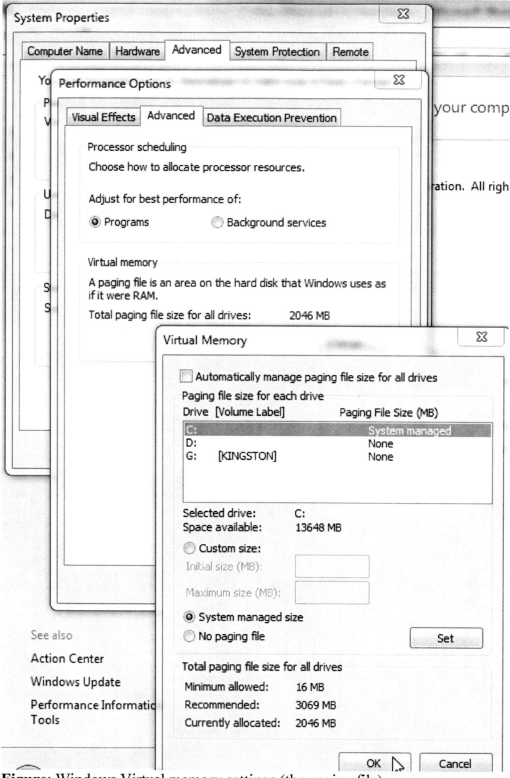

Figure: Windows Virtual memory settings (the paging file)

The paging file can contain references to files, entire contents of files or parts of files even after you have deleted them. Because like any deleted data, the paging file can be recovered and its contents viewed, it poses a privacy threat. It could contain webmail contents, IM chats and even recent passphrases stored in memory.

Unfortunately, the paging file *cannot* be simply selected and deleted as you would a normal data file. The paging file is locked because it is almost always in use and so it cannot be easily deleted.

Instead, you can set up your system to clear this paging file when your computer shuts down. However, be warned that setting up your system to clear the paging file will significantly increase the shutdown time of your computer by as much as a few minutes. For that reason, it is recommended that you clear the paging file every now and then by changing the setting and putting up with a few slow shutdowns, then wipe the free space on your system (see 'Chapter 14: Wiping Your Sensitive Data'), and then revert the setting back.

! Warning !

If you are not comfortable with changing the Registry, please proceed with caution or enlist help because you could harm your computer.

How to Edit the Registry to Clear the Paging File

Start the Registry Editor by entering "regedit" (no quotes) in your Windows start menu, as shown earlier in the 'Accessing the Registry' section starting on page 97. Once in the Registry Editor, select *Edit > Find.*

Now search for the term "ClearPageFileAtShutdown" all in one word with no spaces and without quotes. This is shown in the next screenshot.

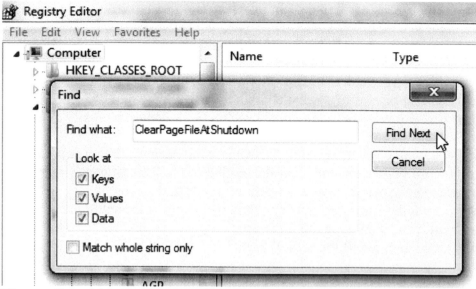

Figure: Searching for the page file clearing setting in the Registry

Once you find the term (as shown below), double-click it.

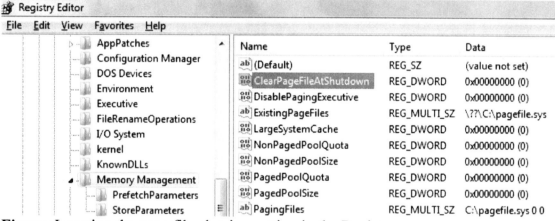

Figure: Locating the page file clearing setting in the Registry

As shown in the next screenshot, change the **value data** from 0 to 1. This turns *on* the page file clearing at shut down.

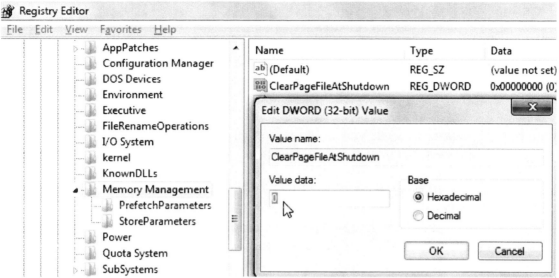

Figure: If the *Value data:* field is set to 0, this means that page file clearing is *switched off*

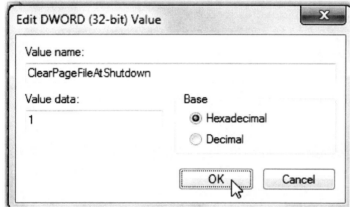

Figure: Setting the *Value data:* field to 1 will *switch on* page file clearing

Continue searching through the entire Registry for the same "ClearPageFileAtShutdown" term in case it appears multiple times. This might happen if you use multiple accounts on your computer, for example. To search for other instances of the same key, use **F3** to 'Find Again' in Registry Editor or go to the menu and select ***Edit > Find Again***.

If you want to go back to *not* clearing the paging file at shutdown, follow the same steps as above but change the *Value data:* back to 0.

Of course, the increased time taken (of up to a few minutes) to shut down is not ideal. An alternative solution is to set up an encrypted or, better yet, hidden operating system because even the PAGEFILE.SYS paging file can be protected by using full disk encryption (see page 163).

Finding and Deleting 'Flash' Cookies

Flash cookies are used by websites that use the Adobe Flash Player for animation, audio or video. Similar to browser cookies (see the 'Records your Web Browser Keeps' section starting on page 74), they store a small amount of data on your computer so the website can recognize you when you return.

Flash cookies are rather insidious because you would reasonably expect that they are deleted when you clear your browser's cookies, but they are not.

To see the Flash cookies on your system, go to the Windows start menu or Explorer bar and type %APPDATA%\MACROMEDIA\FLASH PLAYER\#SHAREDOBJECTS. The %APPDATA% part is simply a reference to where your application data is stored on your computer because the location will vary for each user. For example, C:\Users\Matthew\AppData\Roaming\Macromedia\Flash Player\#SharedObjects\ is one location, but yours will be different. The folder refers to *Macromedia* as opposed to *Adobe* as the Flash Player was originally developed by the former and acquired by the latter.

Figure: Navigate to your Flash cookies in the Explorer bar (shown) or the Windows Start menu

You should now be at the folder(s) containing your Flash cookies. Thankfully, they can be deleted like any other files or better yet *wiped* (see 'Chapter 14: Wiping Your Sensitive Data' starting on page 173). The next screenshot shows the Flash cookies being deleted.

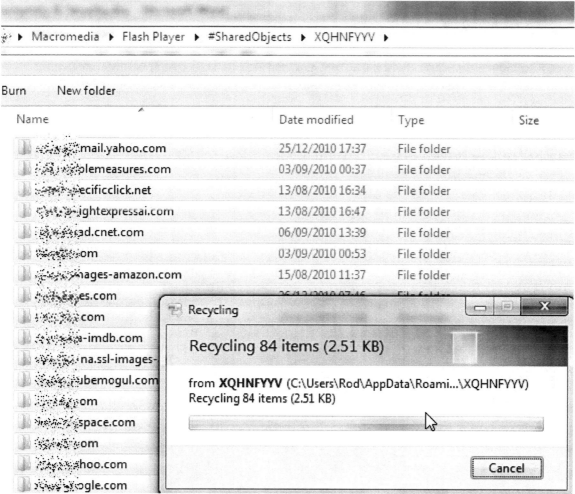

Figure: Once at the listing, you can manually delete the Flash cookies on your system

Recommended Software for Clearing Unwanted Trace Data

The easiest way to clear unwanted trace data from your computer is to use specialist software designed to do that. The following software is recommended at the time of writing.

Premium (Not Free) Software

Privacy Eraser (Pro) (by PrivacyEraser Computing, Inc.)
http://www.privacyeraser.com/download.html

> One of the best privacy protection applications. The software has a clean and intuitive interface. It removes traces from lots of applications, including most browsers, and allows users to set up further plug-ins (see http://www.privacyeraser.com/plug-ins.html) and custom items as well. It also includes strong **data wiping** capabilities.

Figure: A screenshot of Privacy Eraser Pro's main menu

Window Washer (by Webroot Software)
http://www.webroot.com/En_US/consumer-products-windowwasher.html

> Window Washer's built-in features allow you to clear out recently used (MRU) lists in Windows and dozens of applications alike. It can also be configured to delete Registry entries that you specify. You can also tell Window Washer to automatically run at start up, shut down or at intervals of between 15 minutes to once a month.

Free Software

Free Internet Window Washer (by eUsing)
http://www.eusing.com/Window_Washer/Window_Washer.htm

> A simple utility that is equally appealing to novices and advanced users. It enables you to delete unwanted trace data from a wide array of applications and enables expert users to set up and clean custom items.

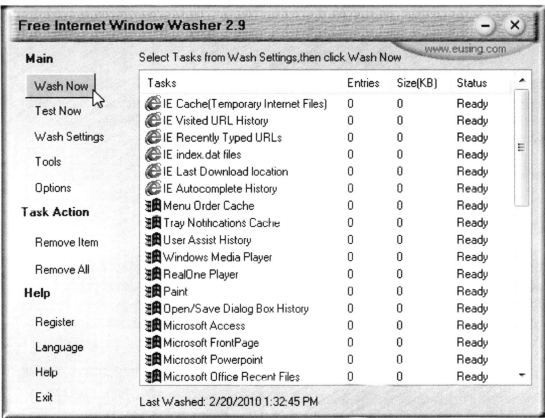

Figure: A screenshot of Free Internet Window Washer's main menu

About Forensic Software

Introduction

If somebody is determined to investigate your computer, they could use specialized forensic software to examine your computer for data, including hidden and long ago deleted files on your hard drives and other storage media. Computers are routinely analyzed by forensic software experts hired for contractual, civil, employment or marital disputes.

Knowing a little bit about how forensic snooping software works will help you to understand why the washing up, data wiping and encryption techniques in this book are so important.

How Forensic Software Experts Go About their Task

The forensic software experts first create an exact physical duplicate of the subject hard drive, called a **disk image** or **bitstream**. An exact physical duplicate means a bit-for-bit copy and therefore includes not only your original data files, but also any hidden data on the drive in places like the Registry, Windows paging and hibernation files, the FAT/NTFS disk indexes, and even bad disk clusters.

More About: FAT and NTFS

FAT and NTFS are acronyms for File Allocation Table and New Technology File System. They are both standards for formatting computer hard drives and keeping track of the files on them. NTFS is the newer standard, introduced with Windows NT and commonly used to format hard drives. These days, FAT is used rarely for newer hard drives but is still commonly used with other storage media such as portable drives or USB sticks.

Sometimes the expert is hired to visit your computer after hours, acquire a copy of your hard drive(s) and examine them later off-site *without you ever knowing*. An identity thief, business rival or other adversary is just as capable of doing this to you.

Typically, the forensic software applications are as expensive as they are sophisticated. The software packages most used by experts can cost in the *thousands of dollars* and require professional training in how to use them. The features of expert-level forensic software include disk image creation and the ability to perform powerful searches of computer hard drives. They can examine deleted files, the names of previously deleted files and folders (called *directory entries*), the Registry, FAT/NTFS disk indexes, file slack and may also include capabilities like file decryption, password cracking and steganography detection. The leading software applications in this field include **EnCase** (by Guidance Software), **Forensic Toolkit** also known as **FTK** (by AccessData) and **Freddie** (by Digital Intelligence).

How to Affordably Examine Your Own Hard Drive

If you wish to get a flavor of what it is like to poke around your hard drive and see what may be detectable and recoverable, you can try the following recommended software at the time of writing.

Directory Snoop (by Briggs Software)
http://www.briggsoft.com/dsnoop.htm

> Directory Snoop is not forensic software in the purist sense, but it is a utility that lets you investigate your disk drives at a detailed, technical level. It might not be used by professional investigators, but it is affordable and allows you to see your FAT/NTFS disk indexes, raw clusters, and the names of previously deleted files and folders (directory entries). It also has the ability to purge these directory entries from your computer's disk indexes. Directory Snoop can also be used to recover previously deleted files. This is a superb personal product for both wiping data and ensuring that data has been wiped. It is not free but allows you to have a number of free, trial uses before you must purchase a license.

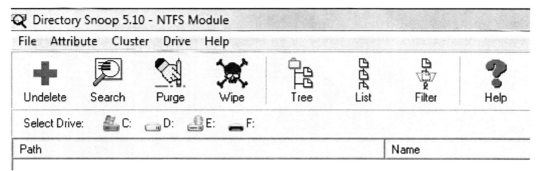

Figure: A partial screenshot of the Directory Snoop software

To see this kind of computer forensic software in action finding sensitive information embedded in the clusters of a hard drive, see the in-depth illustration for advanced users in 'Chapter 14: Wiping Your Sensitive Data' starting on page 173.

Chapter 11: Protecting Your Identity and IP Address with Anonymous Surfing

Introduction to IP Addresses

Although you may feel anonymous on the Internet, this is hardly the case. Learn about IP addresses and then use the techniques here to keep your online identity private.

As described in 'Chapter 10: Covering Your Tracks and Washing Up' starting on page 73, your web browser records every site you visit, every download you initiate, every image or video you view, and every single link that you follow and - unless you have changed your settings (see the 'Records your Web Browser Keeps' section starting on page 74) - keeps a *history*, a record of the websites you last visited.

In addition to the history and 'most recently used' (MRU) lists that record your recent activities, your browser's **cache** saves the actual *contents* of the web pages you have visited. Even when you have cleaned out your cache, the information may still be stored in the cache's index file, the Registry or in directory entries (see page 178). Similarly, Internet website URLs or actual documents or files that you have saved as favorites or bookmarks are easily located on your computer and reveal your activities.

To make matters worse, your online access leaves a fingerprint in the form of an **IP address** - discussed more below. Even outsiders that have no physical access to your computer may still be able to determine your activities, trace and profile you.

Top Tip

Read the privacy policy of your ISP and your other online service providers to make sure that they are respecting and protecting your privacy. For example,
- do they keep logs of your online activities?
- do they share your personal information with third parties?
- do they keep copies of your read emails (emails downloaded from their server)?
- do you have a right to review and correct the information in their possession?

What is an IP Address?

An IP address is a numerical address assigned to any machine with a direct Internet connection. The IP address is in four parts, with the first two parts normally indicating the network, the third part the sub network, and the fourth part the specific machine on the network.

This means that every computer connected to the Internet (or any IP network for that matter) is identified by a unique 32 bit number. IP addresses are usually written in a series of four 8 byte numbers written in decimal and separated by periods (known as dotted quad notation). For example, 151.196.0.0.

Each of the four numbers is in the range of 0 to 255. The number furthest to the left is the most significant. The further right you go, the less significant, but more specific the address. For example, 115.169.57.01 and 115.169.57.02 are right next door to each other while 115.169.57.01 and 116.169.57.01 would be completely unrelated.

IP Address = Your Online Fingerprint

Your IP address 'marks', like a fingerprint, all of your online activities. It attaches to your requests for web pages, it attaches to your email messages, it attaches to your newsgroup posts, and it identifies you while chatting or downloading torrents. With a number of widely available tools, someone can easily track down your activities knowing little more than your IP address. Some marketers *rely* on being able to track and profile you by IP address as their basic business model. Hackers and identity thieves go one step further and may launch attacks against your IP address looking for ways to exploit your system and gain access to your personal information.

This is why anyone who spends time online must do so with privacy, anonymity and security in mind.

If you do not know how to determine your IP address see the **'what is my IP address' links** on page 141 or use the IP address gadget on the www.cogipas.com homepage.

More About: IP Addresses

→ If any of the four 8 byte numbers are outside the range 0 to 255, it is not a real IP address

→ A single machine may have more than one IP address (e.g., a web hosting server)

→ A series of IP addresses may also be shared amongst a pool of machines (e.g., an ISP using a pool of dynamic IP addresses for old fashioned dial-up users)

→ IP address 127.0.0.1 is always your own machine (known as the canonical loop back address)

→ You can sometimes send email to an IP address by using the following syntax: user at [w.x.y.z] (e.g., username@[IP address])

→ The IP addresses 10.0.0.0 to 10.255.255.255, 172.16.0.0 to 172.31.255.255 and 192.168.0.0 to 192.168.255.255 are reserved for *private* IP networks to prevent conflicts with *public* ones. Therefore, if you see any of these IP address ranges it means that the email, post or request was forwarded at some point from an internal network before being routed to the Internet

---

The Privacy Risks

A certain amount of information is automatically sent from your web browsing software to the websites you visit. This information can include your IP address, your geographic location, the pages you previously visited, how long you stayed on a page, the site you came from (called the referring site), the operating system you are using, the information residing in your clipboard from your last cut-and-paste, the web browser you use, and more. Even with this seemingly innocuous information, a profile about you could start to quickly take shape.

Also, malicious websites could use this information to exploit potential holes in your computer system or try to capture passphrases in temporary memory. These same sites could use **malicious scripts** to interact with your computer and attempt to plant malware (this is sometimes called "**drive-by hacking**"). The hackers may go so far as to alter your security settings and start to launch attacks from your computer.

<u>Online Tracking and Profiling</u>

Once someone has your IP address, the identity revealing resources listed on page 141 are the tip of the iceberg in how they can be used to start learning about your identity. If that same party is able to cross-reference enough data and determine for example the websites you visit, your email address (perhaps by using an **email/web bug**), your chat room or Usenet nicknames, a comprehensive profile starts to take shape in no time. Your profile could then be used by hackers, identity thieves or perhaps just annoying Internet marketers or large, data harvesting corporations.

You can protect yourself by hiding your IP address behind a **proxy** or a **virtual private network** (or **VPN**) service – these are covered in detail later in this chapter starting on page 129.

In addition, some search providers can identify the search terms entered by specific users. If you enable Google's Web History feature (http://www.google.com/history/) you can see for yourself that all of your online activities can be potentially recorded and tracked. While for some activities this can be extremely helpful, it does show the possible extent to which an online profile can be built.

Figure: If you enable it, Google's Web History feature will track every site you visit

Further illustrating this point is that in response to thousands of requests for records - for example in response to subpoenas in civil lawsuits - providers like Google and Yahoo can produce lists of users' search histories complete with IP addresses which alone may be more than enough information to track down an individual.

At the time of writing, Gmail's own privacy policy at http://www.google.com/intl/en/privacy/ privacy-policy.html makes clear that "Because of the way we maintain certain services, after you delete your information, residual copies may take a period of time before they are deleted from our active servers and may remain in our backup systems." This suggests that information is potentially recoverable for a long time.

Using a Limited User Account to Surf the Web (and to Minimize Damage by Hackers)

A further layer of protection when surfing the Internet is to do so using a limited **user account** in Windows. User Accounts were discussed in 'Chapter 7: Basic Windows Security' starting on page 51.

If you set up a limited user account *without* administrative privileges and use it for your surfing activities, this should restrict the damage posed by hackers targeting you or by a drive-by hack (when you visit websites that contain malicious software code). The extent of the damage that could be caused by a hacker or by a drive-by hack will be significantly lessened by the restrictions placed on the more limited user account.

The next series of screenshots recap how you set up a limited user account in Windows.

Figure: Accessing the user accounts settings

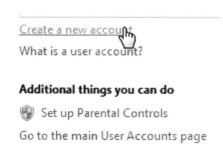

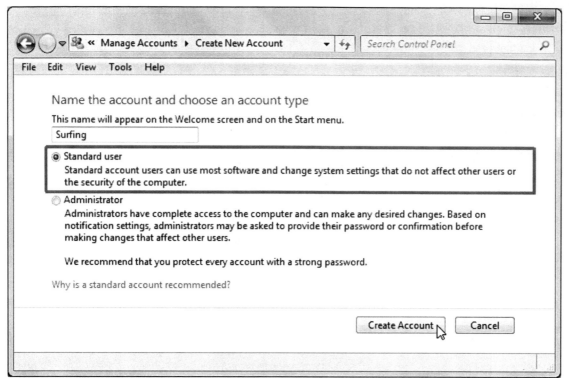

Figure: Setting up a 'Surfing' Standard user account to maximize your protection while surfing the Internet

IP Address Tools

If you are still wondering what IP addresses have to do with web surfing, you need to know a little about how website addresses, or URLs, are converted to an IP address. A **Domain Name System** or DNS for short refers to the process that takes place when you type an URL in your browser. Essentially what happens is:

- Your browser asks your operating system what IP address maps to the URL (e.g., website address) you have requested

- Windows sends this request to your local name server (usually your ISP's name server)

- If someone else sharing the same DNS server as you (e.g., another user of the same ISP) has previously visited the URL, the DNS server may already know to where the URL maps

- If your ISP's DNS server does not know to where the URL maps, it sends the request onto yet another DNS server and so on

- Once the request is answered, your browser is sent the appropriate IP address and visits the corresponding website

Below is a grab bag collection of related IP address tools you may find interesting.

Use a **look up service** to convert a domain name into an IP address. If you only have someone's domain name (e.g., example.com) but want information about the underlying IP address, these tools convert a domain name to an IP address.

- http://www.ipaddresslocation.org/dns-ipaddress-lookup.php

- http://network-tools.com/

- or type "IP address to domain look up" in your favorite search engine

To discover who administers an IP address, perform a **WHOIS** search on the domain name.

- http://www.networksolutions.com/whois/

- InterNIC administers North American-centric domains (e.g. .COM, .NET and .ORG) and their WHOIS search is at http://www.internic.net/whois.html

- RIPE administers European-centric domains and their WHOIS search is at http://www.db.ripe.net/whois

- APNIC administers Asia Pacific-centric domains and their WHOIS search is at http://www.apnic.net/apnic-bin/whois.pl

Some WHOIS searches are also available from third parties.

- http://www.ip-adress.com/whois/

- http://www.webyield.net/domainquery.html

- or type "whois domain search" in your favorite search engine

Lastly, **Intelius Isearch** at http://www.isearch.com/ is a comprehensive collection of online tools you can use to obtain information on an individual based on their Internet or other traits (email address, screen name, phone number or name) - a 'one stop shop' for tracking down someone. The free search will display some basic, enticing information in the hopes that you will pay for a more comprehensive report.

Surfing Anonymously Using a Web Proxy

By using a web **proxy**, you place a separate computer (with a separate **IP address**) between you and the websites you access. If the proxy is functioning properly, the site receiving your web page request will see the IP address of the proxy, and not the real IP address of your computer's connection.

Think of a proxy as a "middle man" server. The IP address of the proxy server will be reported to the sites you visit, rather than your own. This means that any WHOIS-type or other identity digging queries reveal the proxy server's host and country information and do not identify you in any way.

Note that using a proxy does *not* make you fully anonymous (see the 'More About' box below). Many websites claim that proxies make you anonymous but this is not necessarily the case. What a proxy server does is make it more difficult to identify you by your web browsing activities. Instead of the IP address being traced back to you, a proxy server forces anyone trying to determine your identity to obtain the logs from both the visited site *and* the proxy server in-between, which is not an easy task.

You should also remember that the proxy only protects your IP address from the web server to which you are making the request. An eavesdropper (e.g., your ISP) on the communication channel between you and the proxy may see all the information sent and received by you. Note that some online services - especially some webmail - may *not* work through a proxy.

More About: Proxies

Your average over-the-counter anonymous proxy isn't exactly perfectly anonymous. Yes, it may hide your IP address from the websites you visit and may unblock certain websites behind firewalls, but not much more. Your ISP will still be able to determine which websites you visit and, through your ISP, perhaps your employer, government, or anyone else including hackers can get the same information.

Further, the administrator of the proxy can see who you are and everything you're doing through the proxy. This administrator can even substitute websites or inject advertising, viruses or other malware into your online session. In some cases, anonymous proxies are just a quick and easy fix to unblock websites, but not to keep your communications truly 100% private.

For these reasons, consider implementing a **virtual private network** or **VPN** (see the next section starting on page 136). A VPN lets you anonymously connect to websites without even your ISP being able to determine the websites you are visiting. Your ISP or any other potential eavesdropper on your connection will only be able to see an encrypted stream (sometimes called a tunnel) of data between you and the VPN service provider which acts as a proxy.

> **Top Tip**
> You should keep in mind that if somebody wants to find the visitor of a web page or website badly enough and has the resources, they probably can.

Finding a Web Proxy to Use

There are many public proxies available. Sometimes, you can successfully locate proxies by typing "configuring the proxy" in your favorite search engine.

Similarly, there are a number of websites that do this leg work for you and list available proxies. Below, some sites are listed, but please know that by their nature they do tend to come and go. You can always perform a search in your favorite search engine for "anonymous web proxies" or "open proxies".

- http://www.checkedproxylists.com/ (scroll down and then choose a category)

- http://www.workingproxies.org/ (scroll down)

- http://www.textproxylists.com/ (choose a category from the left menu)

Once you have found a suitable proxy, you will need to set it up in your browser software. This is discussed below under the 'Setting Up a Web Proxy in Your Browser' section starting on page 131.

Using a Web Form-based Proxy

Web form-based proxies are easy to use because you only need to visit the page and type the URL into the page's proxy box. They are handy if your activities are not super sensitive, but the convenience also means that you usually have little control over the settings.

- http://anonymouse.org/anonwww.html

- http://www.guardster.com/free/

- http://proxify.co.uk/

- http://behidden.com/

- http://www.publicproxyservers.com/ > Proxy List

Some web from-based proxies not only mask your IP address but also encrypt and hide the URLs you are visiting. This way, your ISP's or employer's logs will display a different site than those you actually visited. For example, instead of the logs recording that your browser visited www.cogipas.com, it could instead look like you visited www.example.com/3d3vZ2lXMuY29t. These web form-based proxies usually use a secure SSL connection and, therefore, the addresses start with http*s*.

- https://www.securetunnel.com/xpress

- https://clearlydrunk.com/

About Proxy Service Providers

In addition to finding and using an *open proxy server*, instead you may wish to use a proxy service provider (usually for a fee). Some services act just like an open proxy while others use software tools that run seamlessly in the background to mask your browser activity. The end result is the same: your true IP address is hidden. See the recommendations later in this chapter.

Of course, relying on a third party as an intermediary in the process requires a high degree of trust. As a result, you should use only reliable services and this is not always easy to determine.

The process of setting up the proxy is the same once you have the right information from your proxy service provider (usually a proxy address and a port number).

Setting Up a Web Proxy in Your Browser

The steps for setting up a web proxy in the Internet Explorer 9 browser are illustrated in the next series of screenshots. The steps are similar for most browsers; the key is to look for *proxy* settings usually associated with your *connection* settings.

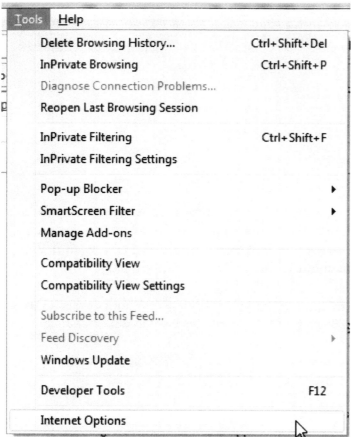

Figure: From the IE menu choose ***Tools > Internet Options***

Figure: Click on the ***Connections*** tab

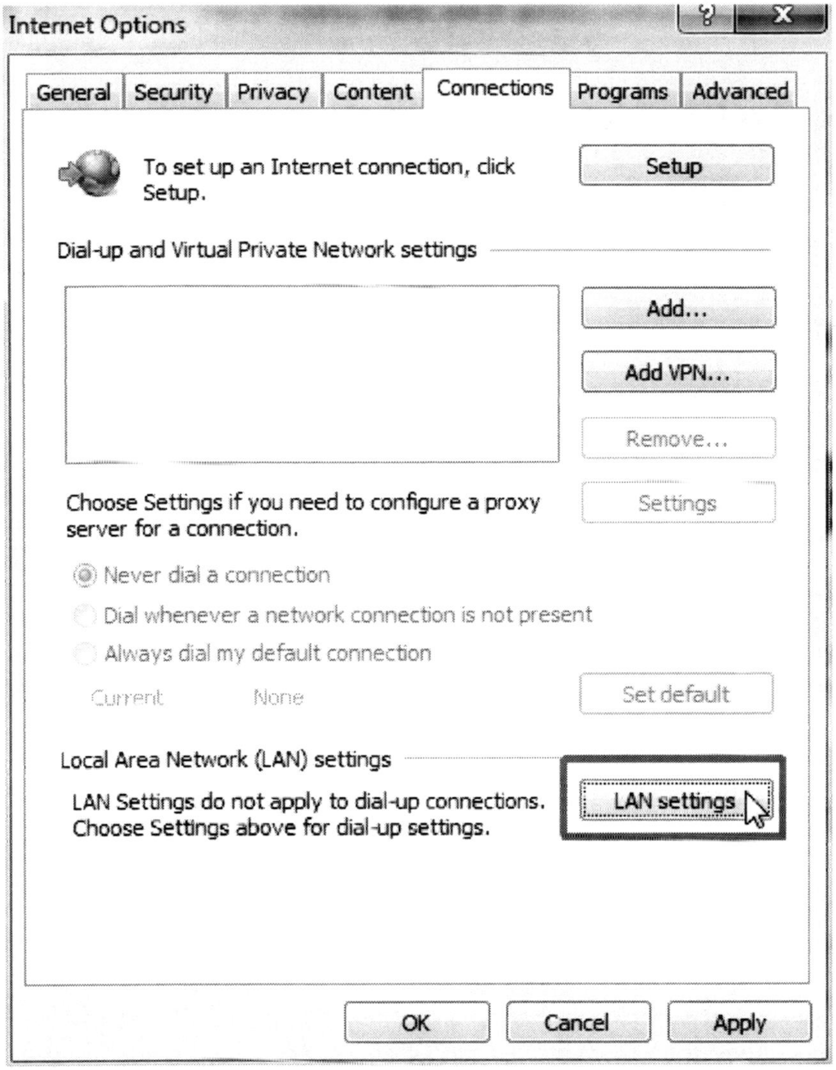

Figure: Click the ***LAN settings*** button

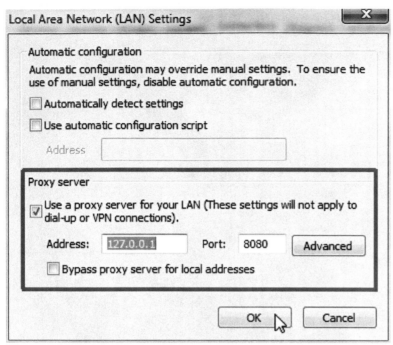

Figure: Now check the *Use a proxy server* box and enter the *Address:* and *Port:* information

The port setting for web browsing is usually **port 8080,** but the instructions found on the site listing public proxies or given to you by the premium proxy provider will tell you.

Always Test the Proxy

Whatever type of proxy you use, you should always check to make sure that it is working properly. The websites in the '**what is my IP address**' section on page 141 outline a number of ways to display your IP address. If these links show the proxy's IP address rather than yours, the proxy is working correctly. You should always check the proxy at the start of any sensitive web surfing session as the proxy could be down, temporarily disabled or not working for other reasons.

In addition, some proxies are **transparent** in nature which means they pass your real IP address to the pages you request. While these proxies should increase the speed of your connection, do not use them for security or privacy purposes. So it is always important to check.

Supported Protocols and Ports

Note that different proxy servers support different **protocols**. Pay close attention to the proxy's instructions and use the proxy for as many protocols as you can. As mentioned above, the usual port for web surfing is **port 8080**.

Some web proxies will also support the somewhat dated, though still useful, **FTP** protocol which uses **port 21**. When supported, this means you can use the proxy's settings in your FTP software for similarly anonymous uploads and downloads to and from FTP servers.

Please note most web proxies will *not* support the **https** protocol (note the "S" on the end) which uses **port 443**. This is the protocol used by your browser to connect to secure pages (e.g., credit card transactions). Virtual private network (or VPN) services are discussed in the next section; *some of them* support the secure https protocol - you need to carefully check the features offered by the VPN provider.

Top Tip
An overview of ports is in the 'Ports Explained - An Introduction' section starting on page 59.

Surfing Anonymously Using a Virtual Private Network (VPN)

Unlike the web proxies just discussed, a virtual private network (**VPN** for short) creates a tunnel of secure data between your computer and the VPN service provider. This can mean that *all* of your connections, including web browsing, peer-to-peer (P2P), chatting and Usenet are channeled through this secure (usually encrypted) tunnel. Anyone snooping your Internet connection (e.g., your ISP) will only see a stream of undecipherable encrypted data. This also makes VPN services a practical solution to the risks posed by public hotspot wireless connections (see 'Chapter 9: Dangers of Wireless Networks and "Hotspots"' on page 63) which are vulnerable to hackers "sniffing" the cyber-airwaves for passwords, credit card numbers and other private data.

Generally, VPNs are superior to web proxies and retain the same benefits, but have other advantages. One downside is that VPN services are usually premium in nature (require a subscription fee) and can be harder to set up. But usually there is only a small program to download which you start-up before you want to "go anonymous." You may have to set up your browser and other Internet software much the same way as for a proxy (see 'Surfing Anonymously Using a Web Proxy' on page 129) by entering into your browser the address and port of the VPN's proxy service.

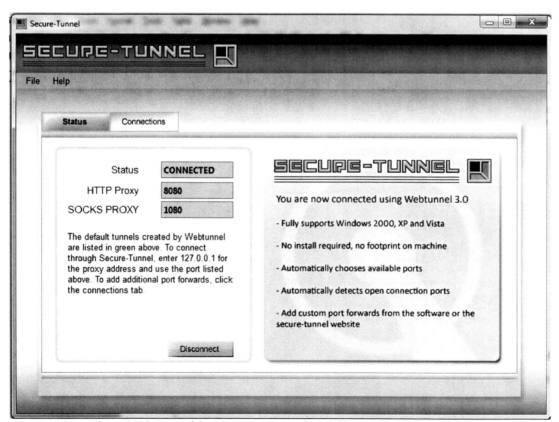

Figure: Premium VPN provider SecureTunnel.com's easy-to-use software

When you visit websites or make other Internet connections (P2P, chat, FTP), the traffic is first routed to the VPN service and then to your computer. Therefore, the VPN's IP address is visible to the computer at the other end of the connection. Your own IP address is kept hidden by the intermediary VPN, acting as a proxy. This also means that all of the subsidiary details obtainable from an IP address - like your geographic location, the pages you previously visited, how long you stayed on a page, the site you just came from (the referring site), the operating system you use, the information residing in your clipboard from your last cut-and-paste, the web browser you use, and more - are also kept safe. Therefore, the VPN keeps your real IP address and the subsidiary information obtainable from your IP address from being disclosed, whether to hackers or overzealous marketers alike.

As with a proxy, you should carefully choose any VPN service. The benefits described above are only as assured as the integrity of the company you deal with. There may also be certain advantages for choosing a VPN service based in a specific country as some jurisdictions have stronger privacy laws than others. For example, Sweden and Canada are often cited by commentators, but always do your own homework.

As an added bonus, a reliable VPN also acts like another line of firewall-type defense as your requested Internet traffic is first being routed through the VPN and, obviously, your VPN's servers are likely protected by hardware, software and human resources that are more advanced than your own.

Testing Your VPN

Once you have connected to your VPN service, you should always make sure it is working properly by testing it, just as you would a web proxy. This is covered in detail later in this chapter's 'Testing Your Proxy or VPN: What is My IP Address' section on page 141.

Recommended VPN Services

Below are some recommended VPN services at the time of writing.

Remember also that you can often use a VPN service for other Internet activities in addition to web surfing; this may include chat and peer-to-peer (P2P) that would otherwise require a separate SOCKS proxy (you will learn about this in the chapters ahead). Check the features of any VPN service carefully as you may be able to get more bang for your buck!

Of course, any reliance on a third party as an intermediary in the process requires a high degree of trust. For example, many services purporting to offer anonymous Chat, IRC and IM state that they are not keeping logs, but who's to say. As tedious as it may sound, you should read the provider's terms of service and privacy policy (usually in the website's 'Legal' or 'Terms of Use' section). Only reliable services should be used and this is not always easy to determine.

VPN Services

SecureTunnel - http://www.securetunnel.com/

> A reasonably priced and stable service that creates an encrypted tunnel of your Internet traffic. What is especially likeable is that the technology (a small program residing in your system tray which leaves no discernible tracks behind on your computer) allows you to use and set up proxies for different functions and applications. For example, you can run an HTTP proxy for your web browsing and *web ripping* (see page 144) as well as a SOCKS5 proxy for *peer-to-peer* (see page 147) or *IRC/IM/chat* (see 'Chapter 17: Chat, IRC and Instant Messaging' starting on page 245). Secure Usenet newsgroup coverage is also offered at a reasonable, bundled price.

Anonymizer - http://www.anonymizer.com/

> Probably the best-known service, Anonymizer has been around for years. Anonymizer is a long-standing and popular proxy service. It is reasonably inexpensive and a free trial is available. Anonymizer is a software installation that acts as a proxy, but only for certain supported software and protocols (i.e., most browsers and port 8080). Anonymizer will mask your IP address if you are using a supported web browser. However, it will *not* mask your IP address if you are using, for example, web ripper software or other non-supported programs or protocols. Therefore, if you are using an unsupported application, you need to use a different proxy. If you are only using your web browser to explore and scour the web, then Anonymizer may be for you. However, if you are using other HTTP-based software, you may need to look for an overall proxy or VPN solution, or use open proxies that, although less convenient, are free.

Perfect Privacy - http://perfect-privacy.com/

Perfect Privacy is a VPN service that provides encrypted Internet connectivity and anonymous access to the web. Users' website requests are sent through the service's encryption and anonymization servers. Data is decrypted and the user's IP address is stripped and replaced with Perfect Privacy's IP address, and then sent to the destination. Responses are also encrypted and sent back to users. Perfect Privacy's servers utilize industry-standard protocols and include SOCKS5 for P2P, chat and instant messaging (all discussed later in this book).

Perfect Privacy's servers cover most of the Americas, Europe and large tracts of East Asia. The service apparently maintains user privacy by not logging information and by providing anonymous payment methods. It offers a large server network, decent server speed and unlimited bandwidth. Free switching between servers, unlimited usage, unlimited bandwidth, decent speed, multiple operating system compatibility, mobile devices compatibility and multiple language support seem to make Perfect Privacy a good value-for-money service.

Strong VPN - http://www.strongvpn.com/

StrongVPN is a well-established US-based VPN service provider that offers a secure encrypted tunnel to connect to the Internet. It also supports Internet connections like ICQ, email and FTP. The user's web requests and data transmissions are anonymized by replacing IP addresses with different American or European IP addresses.

StrongVPN is suitable for high speed surfing, mega uploads/downloads as well as uninterrupted viewing of streaming HD videos due to its high bandwidth network (1 Gbit/s). It provides 24/7 live technical support, and allows a few free server switches per month. Also note that its software is apparently not compatible with some popular firewalls like BitDefender.

Steganos Internet Anonym VPN - https://www.steganos.com/us/products/secure-surfing/internet-anonym-vpn/overview/

Technically, Steganos Internet Anonym VPN is software rather than a service, but with the same result. It provides a secure, encrypted connection to the Internet from servers in Germany. It uses Secure Socket Layer (SSL) for encryption and, consequently, works with SSL enabled browsers. It protects you from ISPs tracking activity and from hackers while using public hotspots. The service also provides anonymity while uploading/downloading data from the web. Steganos Internet Anonym VPN may be suitable for beginners who want an easy solution that provides protection while surfing the web.

Once you have set up your proxy or VPN service, you will need to always test it to make sure it is working. This is dealt with in detail in the next section.

Testing Your Proxy or VPN: What is My IP Address?

Once you have implemented and connected to your proxy or VPN service, you should always test to make sure it is working properly.

The easiest way to test your proxy or VPN is at a number of websites. Some suggestions are listed below. By their nature, some sites and listings do tend to come and go. You can also type "what is my IP address" or "IP lookup" in your favorite search engine.

Visit these sites to make sure that your proxy or VPN is working and that your 'real' IP address is not being revealed. If your proxy or VPN is working properly, these sites should report the IP address of your proxy or VPN rather than your real IP address.

Top Tip

The www.cogipas.com landing page has a 'what is my IP location' gadget, so consider using COGIPAS as your homepage or adding it to your favorites to quickly and easily verify your IP address.

You can also perform a test every time before visiting sensitive websites or accessing your webmail account. Also, remember that any pages you visit on secure sites (i.e., https://...) will normally by-pass your proxy and perhaps your VPN, depending on its features and whether it supports secure SSL connections.

Determining Your IP Address

In varying degree, each of these sites analyzes your Internet connection from a privacy perspective and shows what your browser reveals, including your IP address, when you visit a website.

- http://privacy.net/analyze/ or http://analyze.privacy.net/ (comprehensive but so much so that it may crash your browser)

- http://www.ip-adress.com/ (nice and basic with a location map)

- http://www.ipaddresslocation.org/ (you must scroll through quite a few ads)

- http://antsp2p.altervista.org/ip.php (simple; shows your IP address, nothing more)

- http://www.rexswain.com/httpview.html (shows exactly what an HTTP request returns to your browser)

- http://www.stayinvisible.com/cgi-bin/iptest.cgi (sleek and detailed)

The following IP lookup websites support http*s*

- https://www.securetunnel.com/what-is-my-ip-address (elegant and supports https)

- https://ipcheckit.com/ (bare bones and supports https)

- https://www.metropipe.net/ipspy/ (basic and supports https)

Monitoring Your Ports (Advanced Users)

More advanced users may wish to monitor their active 'ports' to ensure that their Internet traffic is being routed through the proxy or VPN service. Ports are discussed in more detail in the 'Ports Explained - An Introduction' section starting on page 59.

Process Name	Process ID	Protocol	Local Port	Local Port Name	Local Address	Remote ...	Remote Port Name	Remote Address	Remote Host Name	State
firefox.exe	5144	TCP	62444		127.0.0.1	62445		127.0.0.1	AcerLaptop	Established
firefox.exe	5144	TCP	62445		127.0.0.1	62444		127.0.0.1	AcerLaptop	Established
firefox.exe	5144	TCP	62453		127.0.0.1	62454		127.0.0.1	AcerLaptop	Established
firefox.exe	5144	TCP	62454		127.0.0.1	62453		127.0.0.1	AcerLaptop	Established
iexplore.exe	2748	UDP	58877		127.0.0.1					
iexplore.exe	4692	UDP	62445		127.0.0.1					
RIMAutoUpdate.exe	2752	UDP	54200		127.0.0.1					
Skype.exe	3268	TCP	64080		10.0.0.99	10490		189.69.114.75	189-69-114-75.dsl.tel...	Sent

Figure: A screenshot of CurrPorts a free port monitoring utility

A recommended and free port monitoring utility at the time of writing is,

CurrPorts (short for current ports) - http://www.nirsoft.net/utils/cports.html

Port monitoring utilities such as this allow you to monitor the connections made from and to your computer. This is also how a firewall works in the background. Port monitoring utilities let you see which process has opened which port, shows each connection's local and remote IP address, and may even let you terminate a process. Such a utility lets you check that the programs supported by your proxy or VPN service (browser, torrent client or chat program) are in fact connecting through that service's IP address. If you see the proxy's or VPN's IP address in the 'Remote Address' column of CurrPort's display, you can be confident that you are making connections through the proxy or VPN.

Using a Separate Web Browser for Sensitive Activities

Introduction

As Internet Explorer is intertwined with the Windows operating system, you may better maximize your privacy and security by using a separate, stand-alone browser, especially for any sensitive online web surfing. Options include Firefox, Chrome and Opera. Each browser has its own advantages and so it is largely a matter of personal preference which you select, but for privacy features Firefox and Chrome are recommended at the time of writing - please see below.

Using a separate browser is also handy for ultimate security when you install it on an encrypted location on your hard drive or on a completely encrypted (and even hidden) operating system (see 'Chapter 13: Encrypting Your Files to Keep them Safe' starting on page 161). Using two different browsers will best keep your sensitive and non-sensitive web browsing activities nicely segregated.

Recommended Browsers

Firefox Browser (by Mozilla); freeware - http://www.mozilla.org/

Firefox offers excellent protection from spyware and has good privacy features. Firefox's "Private Browsing" mode allows you to browse the Internet without the browser recording the websites you have visited (please see the detailed instructions and screenshots for 'Firefox's Stealth Mode' starting on page 86). The latest version of Firefox also allows you to prevent websites from tracking you; for example, to help you avoid ad-based tracking. Plus, there are lots of excellent, free add-ons available for Firefox to enhance your privacy and security even more.

Chrome (by Google); freeware - http://www.google.com/chrome/

Chrome has good privacy and security features, including built-in malware and phishing protection. When using Chrome's "incognito mode" the browser won't record your recent web pages or downloads to its history list and will delete all new cookies once the incognito window is closed. Chrome also has lots of free "extensions" (add-ons) that you can install to further increase your privacy and security.

Using Web 'Ripping' or Mass Downloading Software

Introduction

Web or site ripping means downloading the content of an entire website to your computer or select parts of the website, for example, based on certain file types (e.g., videos, images, programs or documents). Sometimes it is easier to "rip" an entire site and discard what you do not want than taking the time to *right-click* and **Save File As**... for the downloads you want from the site.

Below are some recommended software products at the time of writing.

As always, if you are undertaking sensitive activities, it is recommended that you use a proxy or VPN. You should also cover any tracks left behind on your computer by the ripping software (see 'Chapter 10: Covering Your Tracks and Washing Up' starting on page 94) and install the software to an encrypted drive (see 'Chapter 13: Encrypting Your Files to Keep them Safe' starting on page 161).

Recommended Software

Premium (Not Free) Software

Internet Download Manager (by Tonic Inc.); about $25, but a 30-day free trial is available - http://www.internetdownloadmanager.com/

> IDM's Site Grabber feature of this software is an impressive mass downloader. An easy, but powerful wizard guides you through the process (shown in the next screenshot). One downside however is that IDM leaves behind in the Registry a lot of trace information about what you download. So make sure that you create some custom wash items for IDM in your covering tracks software (see 'Chapter 10: Covering Your Tracks and Washing Up' starting on page 94).

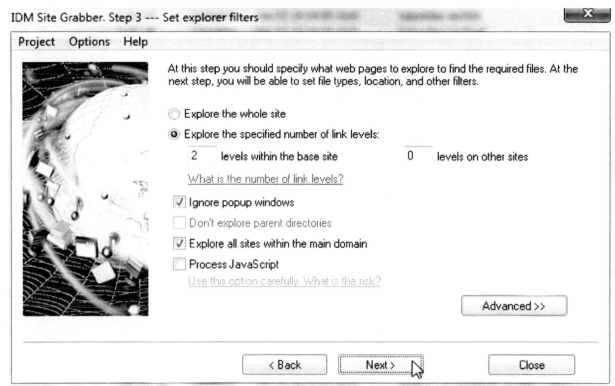

Figure: IDM's Site Grabber feature is a flexible and an easy way to "rip" website content

Free Software

HTTrack Website Copier (by Xavier Roche and other contributors); open source -
http://www.httrack.com/

> HTTrack is a powerful and free web ripper. The FAQ
> (http://www.httrack.com/html/faq.html) and detailed information about filters
> (http://www.httrack.com/html/filters.html) are helpful, especially if you are seeking to
> download particular file types from a website.

Chapter 12: Getting Downloads Using Torrents and Peer-to-Peer (P2P)

Introduction

Torrents and peer-to-peer (or "P2P") are one of the newest, but fastest growing sources of downloads on the Internet. This chapter will outline the risks of using P2P and how to keep yourself private and secure including with some recommended P2P software and torrent tools.

In addition, although it is more difficult to be anonymous using P2P, proxy services can help. You will learn about SOCKS proxy for P2P.

Keeping Secure Using Peer-to-peer ("P2P")

Introduction

It is estimated that a whopping 50% to 75% of all Internet traffic is now "peer-to-peer" (or P2P for short) traffic. Even if you do not recognize the term P2P you may recognize the names of certain current or former P2P software applications, protocols or networks such as BitTorrent, KaZaA, Morpheus, μTorrent, LimeWire, iMesh, BearShare, Gnutella, or the one that jumpstarted it all, Napster.

P2P software allows users to share and exchange data dynamically, with little or no central control. Unlike the process of uploading and downloading data to the web, P2P applications allow users to search and download files directly from a distributed network of users' computers, often seamlessly in the background. The whole process is made even more flexible and easy by powerful **torrent search sites** that allow you to find downloads among literally many thousands of computers at the same time.

Understanding the Risks

Of course this has some privacy and security implications, but if used correctly the benefits of peer-to-peer file sharing can outweigh the risks.

At the outset, you must appreciate that it is more difficult to be anonymous on P2P. As a result, it is best to first examine the various risks to be wary of.

<u>Lots of Malware</u>

P2P provides a fertile ground for people to circulate viruses, worms, Trojans, rootkits and other malware that may do damage to your computer.

Only run executable files (i.e., only click on files that end with *.EXE or *.COM extensions) if you are 100% sure it is all right to do so. Robustly scan all P2P downloads before handling them. Some mischief-makers will circulate malware or other malicious software code under the guise of downloads with pleasing filenames with the goal of trying to trick you into downloading and running them.

Copyright Implications

Some industries are cracking down on copyright infringers, and P2P networks are a growing target for such action. If you share copyright materials, *even by accident*, you could face certain legal risks. For example, some countries' laws can force your Internet Service Provider (ISP) to reveal your identity. Sometimes this can happen in response to a court application that you may never had any notice or chance to respond.

As stated in 'Chapter 1: Introduction', this book assumes that you are using the Internet and all its various tools, including the web, email, Usenet and P2P, for legitimate, non-copyright infringing uses. You should obtain and share your downloads responsibly and legally.

Too Easy to Share

It is so easy to share files using P2P software that many people inadvertently share their private or personal data without even knowing about it. When setting up your P2P software or specifying computer folders to share, make sure there is no personal or private data anywhere in that folder or any of its subfolders. A common mistake is to share your 'My Documents' folder, but that is a recipe for disaster. Imagine strangers anywhere in the world accessing your personal correspondence, diaries, email Inboxes, or perhaps even credit card information, insurance records or tax returns! In the wrong hands, this could lead to outright identity theft and fraud.

Some fraudsters count on these errors and spend their time searching for keyword terms in the hopes of turning up such accidentally shared personal data.

Always carefully set the folders you wish to share. It is best to have your P2P collection folders separate and apart from any personal or official files and folders.

Lots of Spyware and Adware

Although this may be less and less of an issue as time goes by, unfortunately some freeware versions of P2P software have a well-earned poor reputation for being bundled with spyware, adware or other unwanted software.

This bundled software is often installed without your knowledge. Some of it tracks information about your online activities and sends it to advertisers or other third parties. Thankfully, there are a number of utilities to strip out any spyware bundled with P2P or other software (see 'Chapter 6: Protecting Yourself from Malware' starting on page 33).

P2P Reveals Your IP Address

Like all Internet communications, P2P inevitably involves the interaction of IP addresses. This means that your computer's location can be determined and tracked down. You may be targeted for complaints or legal action depending on what materials you are sharing. Also, sophisticated hackers after pin-pointing your IP address could try to gain access to your system and delete files, slow down your network access (e.g., with distributed denial of service (DDoS) attacks) or launch further attacks from your system.

What Can a P2P User Do?

To best address the potential privacy and security threats of P2P discussed above, follow these suggestions:

- Exercise caution with your downloads. Files downloaded via P2P are a source of viruses and other malware. Up-to-date virus protection is a must. Only open (i.e., double-click or run) files after they have been fully scanned with your anti-malware software.

- Respect copyright and avoid downloading or sharing copyright materials.

- Choose your P2P software carefully, in order to avoid spyware and adware. The 'Recommended P2P Software and Tools' choices on page 151 may be of assistance to you.

- Set up your P2P software carefully, especially the folders you decide to share. For example, by default some P2P applications automatically share files that you have downloaded. Check the P2P software's settings and confirm your shared folders regularly, especially if other people also use your computer (e.g., a shared family computer).

- Although it is popular to let P2P software run overnight, it is best to close down the software when you are not at your computer using it.

- Use the trusted utilities available. More and more P2P-specific tools and utilities are being developed all the time to help, including spyware-removal tools, firewalls, more secure P2P client applications, encryption and anonymizing tools. Again, the 'Recommended P2P Software and Tools' choices on the next pages may be of assistance.

BitTorrent-based versus 'File Sharing' P2P Software

This section briefly explains the difference between BitTorrent and other P2P file sharing software.

Think of P2P applications in two camps for the moment: BitTorrent-based and the classic file sharing programs that introduced most of us to P2P (such as KaZaA, Morpheus, Gnutella, LimeWire, BearShare, and Napster). The two camps essentially use a different technology. These days, the BitTorrent-based applications are winning out as they are faster, more reliable and efficient, especially for popular downloads such as the OpenOffice software suite.

In addition, the classic file sharing applications have bandwidth and other limits whereas torrent uses Windows' built-in networking capabilities to spread the "load" among all the computers that are linked (collectively called a **swarm**) to a specific torrent payload. In the result, BitTorrent uses bandwidth more efficiently and completely.

BitTorrent-based applications share files in even their smallest partial pieces even before they are fully downloaded. In contrast, most of the classic applications wait to share the file until it is completely downloaded on a user's system. BitTorrents link up everyone sharing a file (or parts of it) and assigns segments to be uploaded and downloaded amongst them. Many small bits are transferred from many different sources at one time (again, the concept of swarming). So, the more users focused on a single download, the faster the transfers are for it because each participating system is responsible for smaller parts of the file.

However, this can also mean that rare or unpopular files (i.e., those not being shared by many users) can be slower to download as BitTorrents than with a classic file sharing application. This is why some users continue to use both BitTorrent-based *and* classic file-sharing P2P software.

Some commentators also believe that the classic file sharing networks tend to have more fake or "drone" files than BitTorrent-based sharing. Finally, BitTorrent-based applications are (so far) generally freer of spyware or adware.

Recommended P2P Software and Tools

Make sure you read the earlier P2P sections in this chapter so that you understand the various privacy and security risks of using P2P.

Warning

Please remember that, although P2P file sharing technology is itself legal, some or even many of the media files being traded are copyright material. Downloading copyright material could expose you to a civil lawsuit (i.e., being brought to court and asked to pay damages - money - for copyright infringement), including aggressive class-action type lawsuits brought by well funded industry associations. P2P use does not have to be synonymous with copyright infringement so use it responsibly and legally.

Not every P2P software application is listed here. Rather, a manageable, unbiased list of P2P software applications and tools is provided.

P2P Software

BitTorrent-based Software

If you are wondering, what is the difference between BitTorrent based and file sharing networks see the 'BitTorrent-based versus 'File Sharing' P2P Software' section on page 150.

> **μTorrent** (called micro torrent) - http://www.utorrent.com/ - small and sleek, this is torrent application is as excellent as it is popular. One tip: experience shows that, unless you are an advanced user, you should stick with the settings automatically determined by μTorrent as fiddling with them only seems to worsen your download speeds.

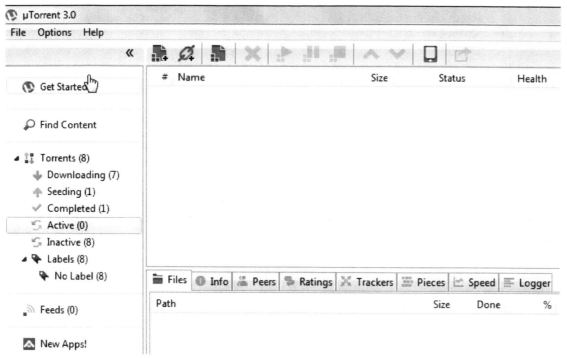

Figure: A screenshot of the μTorrent P2P software

File Sharing-based Software

This still popular family of P2P applications are sometimes called 'mp3 finders'.

> **FrostWire** - http://www.frostwire.com/ - an open source, Gnutella-based client (Gnutella is a type of file-sharing protocol). Easy to use and now supports BitTorrents.

Torrent Search Engines (aka Torrent Indexes)

Almost as important as the P2P software you use are the search engines that you utilize to find torrents. These torrent search engines are also known as **torrent indexes**.

> **Clear-bits** - http://www.clearbits.net/ - distributor of high quality, open-licensed media downloads

> **ISOHunt** - http://isohunt.com/ - a popular torrent search engine with an active P2P community sharing comments and ratings

> **MiniNova** - http://www.mininova.org/ - includes a simple, but good search

If you are blocked from accessing any of these sites or other torrent indexes (e.g., by your ISP or by your geographic location), try accessing them through a web form-based proxy (see the 'Using a Web Form-based Proxy' section starting on page 130) or through a foreign-based proxy or VPN service as you will appear to be accessing them from a different un-blocked IP address location.

More About: Trackers

Not to be confused with *torrent indexes* which are search-like websites displaying available torrents, **torrent trackers** are computers that co-ordinate torrent downloading behind the scenes by matching downloading and uploading peers. Remember that with P2P you almost simultaneously upload while you download and vice versa; this is why groups of peers are called *swarms*. *Trackers* can be *public*, sometimes called *open trackers*, which are available to all; whereas other trackers are *private trackers* which often require registration or operate on an invitation-only basis to keep out unwanted elements.

IP Blocking Tools

This family of tools are useful to P2P users and work somewhat like firewall software by helping to prevent undesirable IP addresses (e.g., known spammers or sources of spyware) from connecting to your computer. These tools should help cut down on fake torrent payloads that, for example, may contain advertising or malware.

> **PeerBlock** (by PeerBlock LLC); freeware - http://www.peerblock.com/ - PeerBlock comes with a set of default libraries of undesirable IP addresses and automatically keeps them up-to-date. At the same time, the block lists are also fully user-configurable should, for whatever reason, you need to tweak the settings and permanently or temporarily allow a blocked site. PeerBlock is an effective tool to help protect your system. A screenshot of PeerBlock follows.

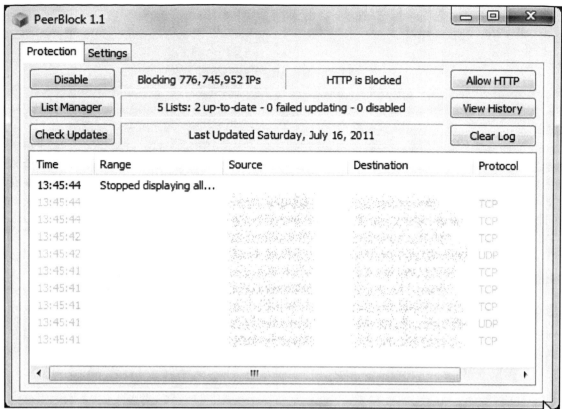

Figure: PeerBlock helps protect your computer and control what IP addresses connect to it

Selecting the Best P2P Privacy Settings

There are a number of reasons why you may wish to keep your torrent traffic private. These reasons include nosy ISPs that may be tempted to monitor or **throttle** (limit) your P2P Internet traffic.

The screenshots that follow are for the recommended P2P software μTorrent. While settings and preferences vary between software applications, you should aim to implement as many of the following strategies as possible in whatever P2P software you use.

- **Encrypting your transfers**. If you have the option of simply *enabling* versus *forcing* encrypted transfers, *forcing* is the safest option and means that you will only connect with other peers that are similarly encrypting their transfers. *Forcing* ensures transfers are encrypted in both directions, but will limit your available pool of peers and result in potentially longer download times or availability issues. Merely *enabling* encryption will allow more peers to connect to you, but will make your traffic more susceptible to detection and throttling.

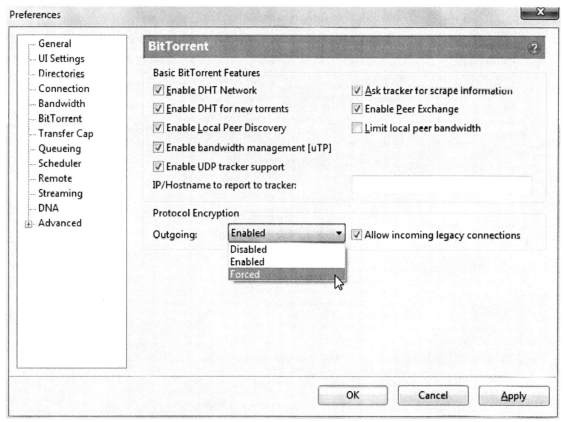

Figure: Selecting µTorrent's Protocol Encryption settings

- **Connecting through a Proxy**. You can route all of your P2P traffic through a third party proxy to help keep snoops from detecting, identifying and throttling your activities. Proxies for P2P - usually SOCKS proxies - are discussed in more detail in the next section.

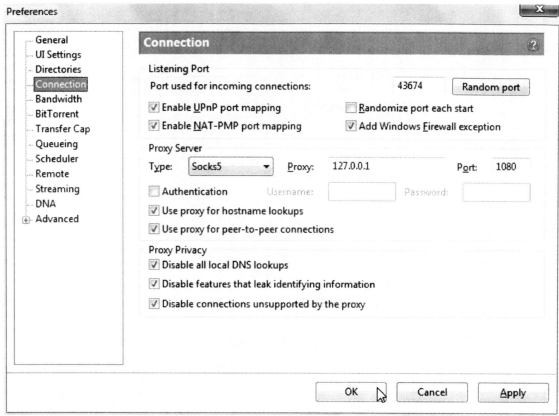

Figure: Selecting μTorrent's Proxy Server settings for a SOCKS proxy

- **Enabling Lazy Bitfield** (Advanced Users). If your P2P software supports it, enable the Lazy Bitfield feature. This keeps hidden - including from ISPs or snoops - the distinct handshake that the BitTorrent protocol uses while "seeding" files (i.e., while making downloads available).

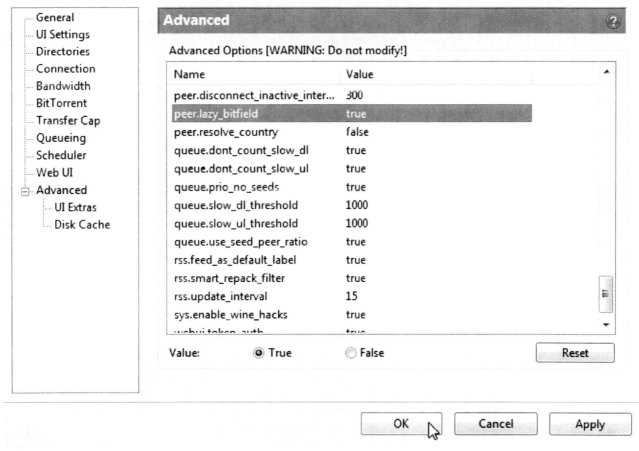

Figure: Enabling µTorrent's Lazy Bitfield setting

Anonymous P2P via a SOCKS Proxy or VPN

Introduction

It is more difficult to be anonymous using P2P compared to web surfing. However, there are services which can add a layer of protection. Generally, these are dedicated SOCKS proxies or virtual private network (VPN) providers that support the SOCKS proxy protocol. Once signed up to either type of provider, you merely need to enter the correct settings in your P2P software.

SOCKS is the name of a proxy protocol and derives its name from the fact that it uses *sockets* to keep track of individual connections. Sockets are how computer networks communicate and that is all you need to know about them for this chapter.

As with a web (HTTP) proxy, a SOCKS proxy for P2P places another server between you and the computers you connect to. This means that the peers you connect to will see transfers to and from your proxy rather than your actual IP address. This adds a level of protection against snoops and profilers, but may result in a drop in your connection speeds. Connections speeds vary between proxy services and can depend on a number of factors including the technology used, the overall load, and the geographical distance from your location, so choose your proxy carefully.

Generally speaking, you are probably better served by signing up to a comprehensive VPN service whose offering includes SOCKS proxy support for P2P.

Of course, any reliance on a third party acting as the middle-man in the process requires a high degree of trust. For example, many services purporting to offer P2P anonymity state that they are not keeping logs, but who's to say? As boring as it may sound, you should read the provider's terms of service and privacy policy (usually in the website's 'Legal' or 'Terms of Use' section). Only reliable services should be used and this is not always easy to determine. As mentioned before, there may be certain advantages to choosing a VPN service based in a specific country as some jurisdictions have stronger privacy laws than others (for example Sweden and Canada are often mentioned by commentators).

Anonymizing P2P Services

SecureTunnel.com (by SecureTunnel) - http://www.securetunnel.com/

This is a reasonably priced and stable service that creates an encrypted tunnel of your Internet traffic. What is especially likeable is that the technology (a small program residing in your system tray which leaves no discernible tracks behind on your computer) allows you to use and set up proxies for different functions and applications. For example, you can run a SOCKS proxy for your *peer-to-peer* and *IRC/IM/chat* (see 'Chapter 17: Chat, IRC and Instant Messaging' starting on page 245), and an HTTP proxy for your web browser and *web ripping* (see page 144).

Secure Usenet newsgroup coverage is also offered at a reasonable, bundled price. Experience with the support team has been good.

BTGuard (by Netcrawled LLC) - http://www.btguard.com/

BTGuard.com appears to be an attractive P2P privacy protection service. It purports to act as a proxy for your torrent traffic and works with P2P software, including the recommended μTorrent. BTGuard is also relatively inexpensive. Sign-up and payment are also quite easy.

TorrentPrivacy - https://torrentprivacy.com/

TorrentPrivacy provides software that creates a secure tunnel using strong encryption for your torrent traffic to pass through anonymously. Anonymity is provided by replacing the user's IP address with those of TorrentPrivacy's servers. It also offers a web proxy for anonymous access to torrent search sites. Other Internet traffic (e.g., email, chat, Usenet) is not encrypted. In other words, the service caters to P2P users. The service states that it ensures privacy by not maintaining any logs. Apparently, it also does not limit bandwidth.

The software seems easy to install and simple to use. Payment options include credit card and PayPal. TorrentPrivacy seems a good option for P2P users who wish to stay protected and increase their anonymity.

HideMyTorrent.com - http://www.hide-my-torrent.com/

HideMyTorrent is a service that will anonymize and secure users' torrent traffic using a real time proxy. It strips the user's IP address and replaces it with that of its own servers for all torrent file requests and uses a custom algorithm for encrypting traffic. The service states that it ensures that ISPs cannot detect or track P2P activity. The software is easy to install and works with out-of-the-box torrent software such as μTorrent, BitTorrent and BitComet.

The servers are all located in the Netherlands and support speeds up to 100 Mbit/s. However, actual speeds will depend on how far the peers you are connecting to are located from the servers. HideMyTorrent states that it does not log server activity and does not store user information. It supports anonymous payment options and the service also offers free trials so you can make sure you are satisfied before actually subscribing.

Chapter 13: Encrypting Your Files to Keep them Safe

Introduction

In this chapter you will learn how to keep the files and data on your hard drive private, safe and secure using strong encryption. You can think of these techniques as keeping your files and data hidden inside an almost impenetrable safe to which only you have the combination.

This chapter explains why everyone should be using encryption and then shows you how to use on-the-fly encryption to protect your computer and keep your information secure. Some recommended applications for encrypting your files and hard drives are outlined as are some handy tips regarding using encryption with portable drives and memory cards.

A number of important guidelines about the importance of good passphrases are also discussed as encryption is only as good as the passphrases that you use. Follow these guidelines to stay protected.

Keeping Your Data Secure

Everyone should use encryption for no other reason than to protect your data in the event your computer is stolen, especially laptops. There are over 600,000 laptops stolen every year in the United States alone!

If you use strong and reliable encryption methods and take some other rudimentary precautions, your security measures will be virtually insurmountable even by all the might and resources available to well-funded adversaries. Or maybe you are crossing borders and do not want any foreign agents snooping your sensitive data.

Business owners and entrepreneurs should also keep in mind that they may have a legal duty to protect certain client or patient information in their possession from unauthorized disclosure. The laptop stolen from the back of your car could cause you many problems if it contained confidential customer information that fell into the wrong hands or was leaked.

Most encryption programs will leave some trace of their presence on your computer so the fact that you are using encryption will probably be apparent. Of course, the very fact that you are using encryption software - or for that matter the presence of proxy, washing, file wiping or other tools and techniques discussed in this book - may raise questions or bring unwanted attention. That said there are enough global concerns about privacy and security these days - just check the Technology headlines in any national newspaper - to answer any such potential criticism or questions.

Using BIOS Passwords

Many computer's Basic Input/Output System (or BIOS for short) allow you to set a boot password so that when your computer boots up, you are asked for a password. If the correct password is not entered the computer will not complete the boot process and start Windows.

Although a BIOS password is nowhere as good as encryption, especially full disk encryption, it is better than nothing and adequate for some users.

To get into your BIOS settings you usually need to press F1, F2 or F8 on your computer within a few seconds of turning on the power. Check your manual for the exact key or, if you watch closely, you may see a quick flash of this instruction on your screen in the first few seconds after turning on your computer.

Once you press the right key at the right time, you will be presented with a BIOS menu which will vary by manufacturer. However, the password feature should be easy to locate and set.

Although setting a BIOS password will provide some protection - especially from unsophisticated adversaries - it can be circumvented. Sometimes the BIOS can be reset to its original non-password protected configuration by changing jumpers or other switches physically located inside the computer. Though not easy, removing the entire disk and reinstalling it in another computer can also be a way to work around and circumvent a BIOS password.

While a BIOS password affords some protection, clearly encryption is a much better option. This is described in detail a little later in this chapter.

A Quick Reminder about the Importance of Passphrases

Your protection - whether through a BIOS password or full-fledged encryption software - is only as effective as the passphrases that you set them up with.

Computer forensic experts are trained to 'crack the easy passwords first' as many people use the same or similar passwords for all of their passphrase needs. Hackers and snoops similarly exploit the fact that many people repeat the same passphrases or only alter them slightly each time.

If you follow the detailed guidelines in 'Chapter 3: Importance of Good Passwords and Passphrases' starting on page 23, a brute force dictionary attack will simply take too long to overcome your passphrase protection. The snoops and hackers will move on to an easier victim.

Best Solution for Privacy and Security: Encrypted Virtual Drives (EVD)

The single best way to protect and keep your activities private is to use on-the-fly data encryption. This ensures that all of your activities, whether downloading files, viewing media downloads, doing Internet searches, chatting online or running programs are done on an encrypted virtual drive (or **EVD** for short).

How Encrypted Virtual Drives (EVD) Work

You create a **container file** on an existing hard drive or portable storage device with a specific **passphrase**. Most encryption software makes this easy; it only takes a few clicks of the mouse once you determine how large a container you want and where you want it stored. The software will create a single file of the size you specified on the drive you selected, whether the location is your computer's hard drive, a portable hard drive, a USB stick or even an SD memory card (the kind used in digital cameras).

It is inside this single container file that the data you wish to encrypt will be absorbed and hidden within, protected by strong encryption. Once you enter your passphrase into the encryption software, the software "mounts" the container on your system. **Mounting** means that the container file becomes unencrypted and that you can access the data stored within it. Saving, deleting, copying and moving data from the (now unencrypted) container is easy. Once the passphrase has been entered, the container shows up as a new drive letter on your system and operates like any other drive on your computer. You can manipulate data on it just as you would any other storage device. Once the container is mounted, the process works exactly the same as plugging a USB stick into your computer. The new drive letter 'pops up' and the data on it can be accessed. This mimicking of a portable storage device is why EVD stands for encrypted *virtual* drive.

This "virtual drive" will only mount with the passphrase with which you created it. As mentioned, once mounted the virtual drive acts like a normal drive: not only can files can be saved to it, but programs can also be installed and run from it. Without the correct passphrase, everything contained on the virtual drive (in the container file) will be totally inaccessible and protected behind strong encryption.

You can and should keep your downloads and anything having to do with your sensitive information on an encrypted drive. When you are done, you dismount (i.e., re-encrypt) the drive, its contents now safe from prying eyes. Until the passphrase is entered all your data is sealed in an encrypted mass of data that will be meaningless to any outsider and even forensic software analysis.

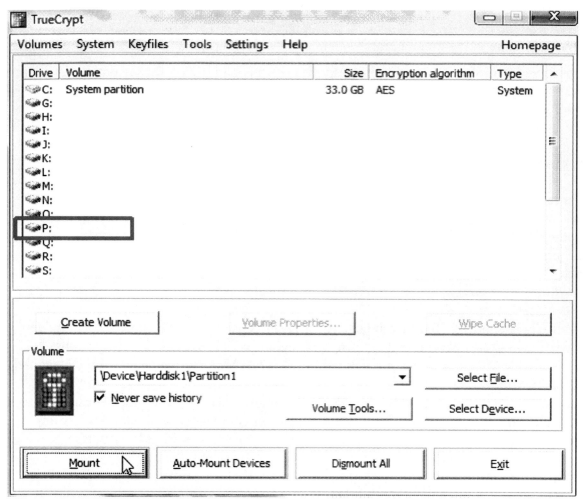

Figure: Mounting an encrypted container as a virtual drive, here as P:, is easy with the right software

With some software (see 'Recommended Encryption Software' on page 167), you can also encrypt your *entire* operating system, covering all your computing activities right from booting up the computer. This involves a few more steps and requires that you read the software instructions carefully. But doing this has the added advantage of encrypting all of the inner "guts" of your computer including its FAT/NTFS disk indexes, Registry, disk cluster information, directory entries, log files, and other sources of trace data that you were shown in 'Chapter 10: Covering Your Tracks and Washing Up' starting on page 94. Encrypting your entire operating system in this way prevents these potential sources of trace information from being discovered or analyzed when your operating system remains dismounted and encrypted.

With some encryption software, it is possible to set up a hidden container or even an entire **hidden operating system** by "hiding" one encrypted container inside another. Needless to say, only advanced users should consider setting up hidden containers or a hidden operating system.

Installing Sensitive Software on Encrypted Virtual Drives (EVD)

Using Encrypted Virtual Drive (EVD) technology also helps to minimize the risks posed by issues previously discussed like most recently used (MRU) records, temporary, autosave or *.INI files (again, recall 'Chapter 10: Covering Your Tracks and Washing Up' starting on page 94). As the latest EVD software can handle encrypted containers as large as today's largest hard drives, you should have enough capacity to accommodate your sensitive data *and* to install on the EVD the software related to your sensitive activities.

Caveat: Encryption is Not Foolproof

However, even this superior EVD encryption method is not foolproof. Unless you choose to encrypt your entire operating system, a number of risks still exist even when using EVD technology:

- any web browsers installed to non-encrypted locations on your system will reveal your web surfing history, cache, cookies, bookmarks and favorites

- recoverable data may remain in your *Windows paging* (or swap) file and FAT/NTFS disk indexes, including empty directory entries (i.e., old file and folder names; see page 178)

- most recently used (MRU) entries may remain in the *Registry* located on your *un*encrypted system or C:\ drive

- applications and compound files may 'leak' data to unencrypted locations elsewhere on your system (unless you remedy this risk with a separate utility like www.sandboxie.com)

- temporary or autosave files may be left behind by applications in the *Windows Temp* folder or other locations on your *un*encrypted system or C:\ drive

As you can see from the list above, even EVD users must implement strategies to get rid of sensitive trace data such as Registry values, empty directory entries (see page 178) and other items that leave traces of your activities. In other words, your sensitive activities may still be revealed or discoverable even if you use encryption. For these reasons it is strongly recommend that you also use **washing software** for your computer - see 'Chapter 10: Covering Your Tracks and Washing Up' starting on page 94.

Similarly, some programs - like Internet Explorer - may integrate with your operating system to such an extent that they cannot be separately installed to an EVD container. Other browsers may pose different privacy risks as they are closely connected to their related toolbars or affiliated website portals. The solution: install and use a **separate browser** (see page 143) on your EVD for your sensitive web surfing. This way, you gain the *convenience* of being able to use the history, cache, cookies, bookmarks and favorites for your sensitive activities, but with the *protection* of having them safely tucked away on a separate, encrypted container.

See the detailed examples for advanced users in the next chapter, 'Chapter 14: Wiping Your Sensitive Data'. Those examples serve to illustrate the insidious nature of trace information remaining on your system and show how data can become embedded in your computer and be difficult to get rid of. Don't risk having your privacy breached by the snooping techniques illustrated in those examples.

Recommended Encryption Software

Below are the recommended applications and tools for encrypting your individual files or your entire hard drives at the time of writing, together with some related tips.

TrueCrypt (by TrueCrypt Foundation) free/open source - http://www.truecrypt.org/downloads

> This is a simply awesome application with amazing (online) documentation and tutorials to match. TrueCrypt is as good as any commercial application on the market and allows you to create hidden encrypted volumes and, for more advanced users, fully encrypted (and even hidden) operating systems. Both the software and its related documentary materials at http://www.truecrypt.org/docs are highly recommended.

BestCrypt (by Jetico) about $40 - http://www.jetico.com/encryption-bestcrypt/

> BestCrypt stores your data on encrypted virtual drives (EVD) which are only accessible once your passphrase is entered correctly. BestCrypt uses strong encryption ciphers and is available for a 30-day trial.

Why Passphrases Matter

It is paramount that you use strong passphrases with your encryption applications. Your protection is only as strong as the passphrases you use. Do not be lazy when it comes to passphrases: make them long, a mix of upper-case, lower-case, numerical and symbols.

Refresh your memory about the best practices to use with the detailed discussion in 'Chapter 3: Importance of Good Passwords and Passphrases' starting on page 23.

Different Passphrases for Different Encryption Software

Although inconvenient, it is also recommended that you use a unique passphrase for *each* different software application and account that requires a passphrase. For example, it may not be difficult to crack the password protection features of a zipping archive utility or word processing program. Similarly, your employer or co-workers may have access to certain passphrases you use. Or hackers may crack your passphrases for webmail or other online accounts, perhaps based on information you have posted on social networking sites.

Regardless of how your passphrase is breached, if it is and you use the same passphrase for your strong encryption software, even this strong protection is now vulnerable to being cracked. Because encryption strength varies from program to program, you should employ different passphrases even for each different type of encryption program you use. Otherwise, your encryption practices will only be as good as the weakest link in the encryption strength of *all* the programs you use.

Lastly, some encryption applications are rumored to have "back doors" built-in to them at the behest of governments in the interests of national security. "Back doors" meaning master passphrases that can be used to overcome the encryption application and access the data encrypted with them. Obviously, reliable information about these rumors is difficult to discover and even more difficult to verify or refute.

Portable Drives, Memory Cards and Encryption

Introduction

Portable drives are popular and practical, especially if you have lots of downloads. It is handy to use a portable drive, USB stick, or even a tiny SD memory card as an encrypted virtual drive (EVD). If you do not know what an EVD is, please see the section 'Best Solution for Privacy and Security: Encrypted Virtual Drives (EVD)' on page 163.

EVD technology lets you easily create an encrypted container on a portable hard drive, USB stick or SD memory card. Once mounted, it operates like any other removable drive with virtually no impact on speed or read/write access. You can use an EVD container on a portable drive to shuttle files from one location to another. If a snoop or adversary gets his hands on the portable hard drive, USB stick or memory card, the information on it will be completely undecipherable without your passphrase.

Figure: Using TrueCrypt to create an encrypted EVD container on a 4GB USB stick

Tip: Don't be Obsessed with Capacity

These days, portable hard drives are huge and affordable. It is now quite possible to get a 1.5 terabyte hard drive for a decent price. However, one consideration to keep in mind is the actual degree of portability. Consider opting for smaller capacity portable drives that *do not* require their own power source. Products such as some models in Western Digital's "My Passport" series are still quite sizable at 320 GB but do not require their own power source. You simply plug the drive into your USB port and that's all there is to it. No fumbling around with an extra power cord to plug in.

This is convenient especially if you are using encrypted virtual drive (EVD) technology and shuttling the drive between two or more computers. It is easy to overlook this important factor and be obsessed with the sheer capacity of drives.

Tip: Using Memory Cards

Memory cards are so small and of sufficient capacity now that they are a great way to securely transport data. Just as it is a good idea to take the memory card out of your camera so that your pictures are not lost if your luggage (with camera) goes missing, it is a handy way to transport data generally, especially sensitive data. Memory cards are even smaller than USB sticks, are easy to keep on your person (even in your wallet), and easy to conceal.

Even handier is that memory card to USB adapters are widely available and inexpensive. These make it just a matter of slipping the memory card into the adapter, plugging the adapter into your computer, and then entering the correct passphrase. Upon doing so, the container mounts and you are able to access the data on it just as if you had plugged a normal USB stick into you computer.

Micro memory cards in particular are about the size of your fingernail (see the next screenshot) making them easy to transport and keep hidden, if necessary.

Figure: The small size of SD and micro memory cards (a micro card is shown above) make them ideal for discreetly transporting data. Courtesy of James Bowe at http://www.flickr.com/photos/ 29848680@N08/3601316250

Chapter 14: Wiping Your Sensitive Data

Introduction

Technologically savvy people know that when you delete a file on your computer, it is still recoverable. It's not enough to simply *delete* your data, even if you regularly empty your Recycle Bin. Computer files are easily recoverable using a number of popular utilities. Don't make the mistake of thinking that hitting the delete key is ever enough! Hard drives are now so large that data and information from many years ago may still be recovered in good condition. Learn how to properly get rid of your sensitive electronic information - by *wiping* it.

In Windows, after you delete a file, you can access the Recycle Bin and recover the file by 'undeleting' it (this feature is provided in case you delete a file by accident). But, even when the Recycle Bin is emptied, the file can still be recovered or "unerased" by a number of widely-available software programs and utilities (see page 183).

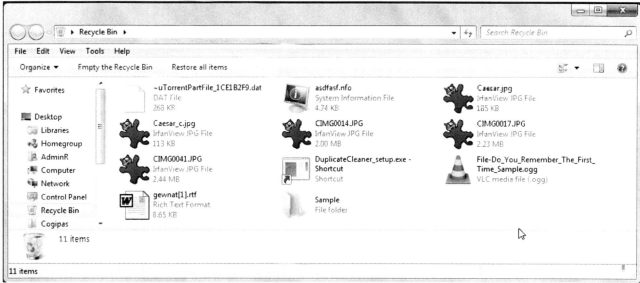

Figure: The contents of your Recycle Bin could represent a privacy risk

What Happens When You Delete a File?

Do not be fooled into thinking that if you delete or overwrite a file or even reformat a drive where data resides the underlying data is gone for good. Whether you try to delete data on your computer by erasing it, changing it or reformatting the volume on which it resides, the information is recoverable.

Your computer's operating system does not actually delete files since to replace (overwrite) every byte of a file takes up precious time. To speed up performance, the operating system basically tells itself to ignore the file in future; something akin to crossing out an entry in a book's index. The operating system 'forgets' the index entry for the old (deleted) file and allocates the physical space on the drive occupied by that file as free for new data. The old data is still physically available on the drive but will (or may) be eventually overwritten with new data on the same physical space. The operating system's act of forgetting is achieved by replacing in the drive's index the first character of the old filename. These drive index entries are called **directory entries**.

In Windows, when you delete a file (by emptying the Recycle Bin), all that happens is that the relevant directory entry for that file in the FAT/NTFS *index* is modified. Windows simply replaces the first byte of the entry in the index and thus ignores the entry in future. This 'frees up' for new data the hard drive clusters that were previously being used by the 'deleted' data. Modified index entries appear as shown in the screenshot below.

1st Cluster ▽	DOS Alias
45379	?XCLUDED.TXT
(45322)	?MAILT~1.TXT
2402	?__LA~1.TXT
(0)	?HOPPI~1.TXT
(0)	?MAILT~1.TXT

Figure: This is what deleted files look like on a hard drive's index using a file recovery utility

The former data is not actually deleted, but remains on the hard drive. Eventually, the same clusters containing the old data may eventually be over-written with different bits and bytes of new data as you add or move files onto that drive. However, given the ever increasing size of hard drives, it could be a long time before these clusters are over-written. So files that you thought were deleted long ago could be discovered and undeleted, often fully intact.

Using a simple data recovery tool, you can see what this looks like in the next screenshot.

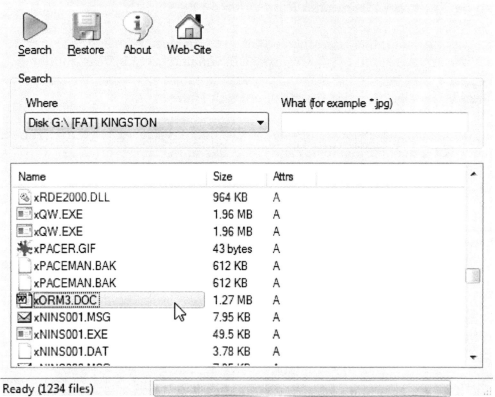

Figure: Deleted files are easily recovered with a file recovery (undelete) utility

So, to recap: deleting a file simply tells the operating system that the physical space the file was previously occupying is now available to be overwritten with new data.

Using a Shredder for Your Data

People will take great care and time to delete sensitive *paper* files. You should apply the exact same logic to your electronic files. If you want to get rid of sensitive electronic files for good - shred them! The equivalent concept to shredding for computer data is referred to as **wiping**.

At a minimum, you should **wipe** (as opposed to merely delete) any sensitive files and data. The difference is that wiped files have been deleted AND the space on the hard drive previously occupied by the data written over many times with random data to ensure that the original file cannot be recovered.

Consult the 'Recommended Wiping Software' section on page 183 to ensure that you are properly deleting your sensitive files. Some file recovery and disk snooping tools are also listed so that you can prove to yourself that your files are beyond recovery.

Sensitive Data can also be Recovered from Your Hard Drive's File Slack

Adding to the risk of recoverable data is that regardless of the size of a piece of data, the operating system always allocates a minimum amount of *physical* space in which to save it. This minimum amount of physical drive space allocated by the operating system is called a **cluster**. Any part of a cluster that is not fully used by the data is called **file slack** or **slack space**.

This file slack or slack space is the space between the logical end and physical end of a file. The **logical size** of a file is the exact size of a file in bytes and is the size of the file reported in Explorer. The **physical size** of a file is the amount of space that the file physically occupies on the disk, which is usually larger than the logical size.

Depending on its size, a disk is divided into thousands or millions of **clusters**. Each cluster is the smallest physical space allocated on your hard drive for saving data to it and, for newer drives, is set to a minimum size of 4k. Older drives have minimum cluster sizes of 16k which results in more 'wasted' drive space.

The minimum physical size of a file on the disk is always one cluster, even if the file is empty and has a length of 0 bytes. File slack results because a file entry always occupies a whole number of clusters even if it does not completely fill that space with its data. When this occurs, the logical end of the file comes *before* the physical end of the cluster - with the remaining bytes being remnants of previous files. These previous remnants in the file slack may include sensitive data.

Think of clusters like empty buckets with your drive being made up of thousands or millions of buckets. If the volume of water you wish to store (or at least the last bucket worth of a large volume of water) is less than the volume of a whole bucket, the last bucket will always have some empty space; this space between the top of the water and the top of the bucket is the file slack or slack space.

This means that any parts of your old (deleted) data that were not completely overwritten by new data are also likely recoverable. In other words, old (deleted) data residing in the slack space of clusters - the nooks and crannies - is also recoverable.

Recall that computer forensic software can easily recover deleted files, sometimes from *years* back; this includes by the forensic software examining data residing in your unused clusters.

Good wiping software will also give you the option to wipe your hard drive's "free space". Wiping your drive's free space ensures that any old, previously deleted files cannot be recovered, including from slack space, as the software will fill and over write *all* the empty space on your hard drive.

Wiping Physical Media

Hopefully, you are not throwing out your hard drives, USB sticks, SD memory cards, CD/DVD-ROMs and Blu-Rays with the regular trash. Not only is this bad for the environment, but it is potentially disastrous for your privacy and security. If a dumpster diving identity thief (see the 'More About' box below) only needs a few bank statements from your trash to make your life miserable, imagine a hard drive or DVD-ROM containing gigabytes of your personal data and records.

More About: Dumpster Diving

A *dumpster diving* identity thief is an identity thief that looks through your curbside garbage for documents containing personal information such as bank or credit card statements.

As a rule, you should always *wipe* the entire contents of hard drives, USB sticks and SD memory cards before you throw them out or sell or donate them to friends, family or third parties.

For CD, DVD and Blu-Ray disks some experts advocate "nuking" them for a short time in a microwave oven, but not everyone is comfortable doing this. It should be adequate (and can be fun) to smash the disk to bits with a hammer after having first wrapped the disk in an old dishcloth to make sure that no fragments get into your eyes or make a mess.

In a commercial context, when media has extremely sensitive data on it a business may consider purchasing or renting specialized equipment to permanently destroy data on hard drives, USB sticks and SD memory cards (called **degaussers**) or to physically destroy CD/DVD-ROM and Blu-Ray disks (called **disk shredders**).

What Even Wiping Leaves Behind: Directory Entries

Introduction

As explained in the *data wiping* introduction starting on page 173, when a file is deleted it is still recoverable because all that happens is that the reference to the file (in the hard drive's FAT/NTFS index) is ignored. As you add or move data on your hard drive the "erased" file may eventually be covered over with different bits and bytes, but often the original data is still intact and recoverable.

Wiping data is the best way to make sure that the data is unrecoverable. However, forensic snooping software illustrates that even when you wipe a file (or folder), the original *filename* (or *folder name*) is intact in the bits and bytes of your hard drive. Filenames and folder names in the disk index are called **directory entries**. The names that remain in the disk index of old, previously deleted files and folders are called **empty directory entries**. While a wiped file or folder may now be gone and unrecoverable, its old filename or folder name remains and may itself lead to a breach of your privacy.

Why Directory Entries Remain

Windows' FAT/NTFS indexing systems treat directory entries (filenames and folder names) the same as files and also treats the *moving, renaming* or even wiping of files or folders the same as *deleting* them.

This means that the original name of a deleted, moved, renamed or even wiped file or folder will appear in its original location in the index with its original name (but with its first character blotted out). Therefore, the intuitive trick of simply renaming sensitive files will not work. In addition, if you thought you were well protected by wiping files after being finished with them or otherwise moving them to an another location, including to an *encrypted drive* (see page 163), this may not always be enough. You can see this for yourself by performing your own test (see the next section). Whether after deleting, moving, renaming or even after wiping, you can still find the file's or folder's original directory entry in the drive's FAT/NTFS index.

In addition, sometimes Windows handles long filenames by spanning multiple directory entries and this can lead to directory entries becoming "orphaned" and never over-written.

Ouch! You may have dozens or hundreds of sensitive old filenames or folder names on your computer. To eliminate the risk posed by these old filenames and folder names (the empty directory entries), the wiping software you use should include a feature to eliminate the old filenames and folder names; a process called **purging empty directory entries**.

However, if you are following best practice and are rigorous about doing all of your sensitive activities from an *encrypted drive* (see page 163), the recoverability of previous filenames and folder names will be much less of a risk. This is because once your encrypted drive is dismounted (i.e., re-encrypted), that drive's FAT/NTFS index and resident data will be encrypted and impenetrable without the passphrase. Detailed information about using encryption is contained in 'Chapter 13: Encrypting Your Files to Keep them Safe' starting on page 161.

About Temporary Files and Filenames

The risk of recoverable old filenames is also a concern for temporary files *no matter what methods you use*. For example, you download an archive of zipped files to your encrypted drive (for maximum security). You unzip the archive and click on a file or two to sample the contents. You may not know this but those files are (depending on your software's Options) probably being temporarily saved and opened from your C:\WINDOWS\TEMP (or similar) folder – recall page 104. Other programs or autosave features may also use unencrypted, temporary locations. This means you must search out and purge deleted names from these temporary locations as well.

Note that if you are downloading any files to a non-encrypted drive, even if only temporarily until you move the downloads to an encrypted location, you will need to purge the record of these filenames from the original drive's FAT/NTFS index.

Hopefully this narration and the in-depth demonstration that follows on page 186 serve to illustrate why you should also purge empty directory entries from your system, even if you carefully use encryption *and* washing software.

Getting Right Down to the Cluster Level of Your Drives (Advanced Users)

Taking this further, consider analyzing your hard drive with **forensic software** (see the 'About Forensic Software' section on page 118) to see what sensitive information is embedded in the drive's **clusters**, the smallest physical spaces allocated on your hard drive to save data to it. Use the software to search your drive's contents for a text string that represents potentially sensitive information.

In the next series of screenshots, a search of a hard drive for the text string "steamy" discovers traces of a document entitled HOT STEAMY LOVE LETTER.DOC.

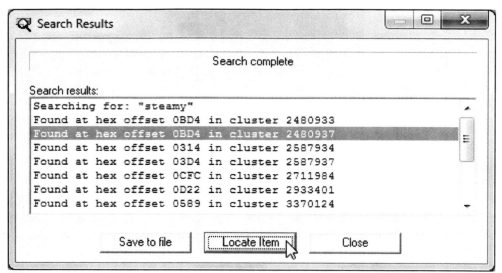

Figure: A search of the entire hard drive is conducted using the text string "steamy"

After the forensic software's search is complete, you can select each search hit to see what this trace data on your hard drive reveals. Depending on the software, you can note the cluster number for any search hit and view the data. In the screenshot below, you will see that the information in and around cluster 2480937 indicates that a document entitled HOT STEAMY LOVE LETTER.DOC once existed on the system.

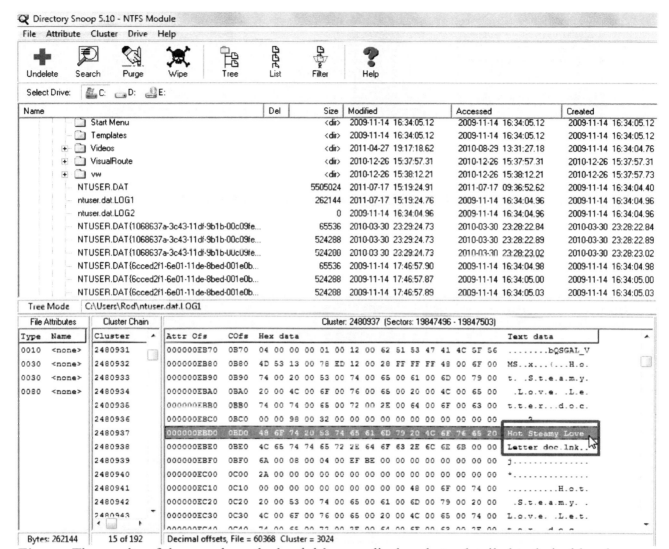

Figure: The results of the search on the hard drive are displayed at a detailed technical level

In this case, the information is contained in a cluster used by the file NTUSER.DAT which forms part of the Windows Registry. But similarly revealing information can just as easily reside and be found in *unused clusters*; that is, data remaining from old, deleted data. As discussed earlier, such trace information can also result from temporary or autosave files, RAM dumps, and as remnants from the Windows paging or hibernation files.

This is why it is important to wipe your drive's free space, but *after* you have **purged empty directory entries** from your system to rid it of records of previously deleted, moved, renamed, and even wiped files and folders.

To recap, the best way to protect your hard drive from privacy breaches is a combination of:

- using disk encryption;

- employing washing software;

- wiping any data you wish to delete permanently;

- purging empty directory entries from your system; and

- wiping the free space on your hard drives.

Recommended Wiping Software

Below are some recommended applications and tools at the time of writing for permanently deleting - *wiping* - your sensitive data.

Data Wiping Software

Directory Snoop (by Briggs Software) about $40 - http://www.briggsoft.com/dsnoop.htm

> Directory Snoop is a utility program that allows you to snoop around your disk drives at a detailed, technical level. This is a superb product that allows you to browse your hard drive's FAT/NTFS disk indexes, wipe data and wipe the free space on your hard drives. It also lets you view the raw clusters and the filenames of previously deleted files (and lets you purge empty directory entries as well) and is a good means for checking that data has been wiped. It can also be used as a general file recovery (undelete) tool. You may use the program for free for a limited number of uses before you are required to buy a license.

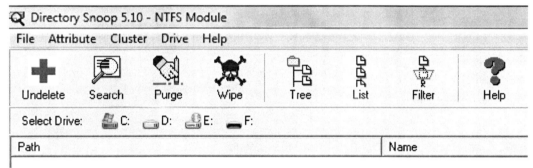

Figure: A partial screenshot of the Directory Snoop software

File Shredder (by File Shredder) free - http://www.fileshredder.org/

> A simple, elegant and decent data wiping utility that is free. It lets you wipe individual files as well as the free space on your hard drive. A screenshot of the File Shredder software follows.

Figure: A screenshot of the File Shredder software

Wipe (by Jetico) about $40 - http://www.jetico.com/wiping-bcwipe/

A utility that properly wipes files as well as the option to wipe free drive space, file slack and the Windows paging file, as well as purge empty directory entries.

Tools for Wiping an Entire Drive

WipeDrive (by White Canyon Software) about $20 - http://www.whitecanyon.com/wipedrive-erase-hard-drive.php

This is US Department of Defense (DoD) approved software for securely deleting the entire contents of a hard drive. It supports all hard drive sizes and formats.

File Recovery (Undelete) Utilities

These tools recover deleted files. You can use them to verify that your wiping methods work.

Directory Snoop (by Briggs Software) about $40 - http://www.briggsoft.com/dsnoop.htm

> Directory Snoop is a utility program that allows you to snoop around your disk drives at a detailed, technical level. It effectively recovers previously deleted files, if the files have not been *wiped* of course.

SoftPerfect File Recovery (by SoftPerfect Research) free - http://www.softperfect.com/products/filerecovery/

> Although not the most powerful tool in its class, this is a simple and hassle-free file recovery tool. It requires no installation and can be executed from a portable USB stick.

Top Tip
Also see the related 'About Forensic Software' section starting on page 118.

Detailed Example of File Wiping and Directory Entry Purging (Advanced Users)

Recall from the 'What Happens When You Delete a File?' section starting on page 173 that when you delete a file it is *not* gone for good. To demonstrate this, the example below will use a straight-forward and widely available utility to recover a deleted file from a USB stick. The example will further show you how to get rid of the old, deleted filename (the relevant directory entry) for good.

For this demonstration, save and *then delete* a file on a USB stick - the example below used a Windows media file (*.WMV) - a video clip - called STRIPPED.WMV. This file could just as easily represent your personal budget, a confidential company report, medical information or whatever else you consider sensitive.

Then, use an undelete software utility to prove to yourself that previously deleted files can be found and recovered, possibly even fully intact.

As you can see in the next two screenshots, the utility easily revealed the existence of the deleted file.

Depending on whether any new data has overwritten the space previously occupied by STRIPPED.WMV (if you need to, go back to page 173 for a refresher about how this works), the file may even be fully recoverable.

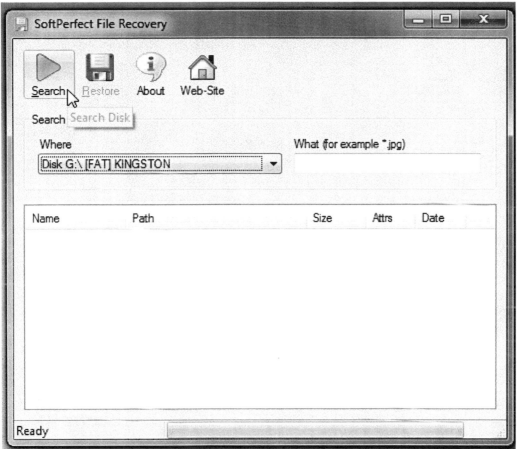

Figure: An undelete utility is used to search the USB stick for deleted files

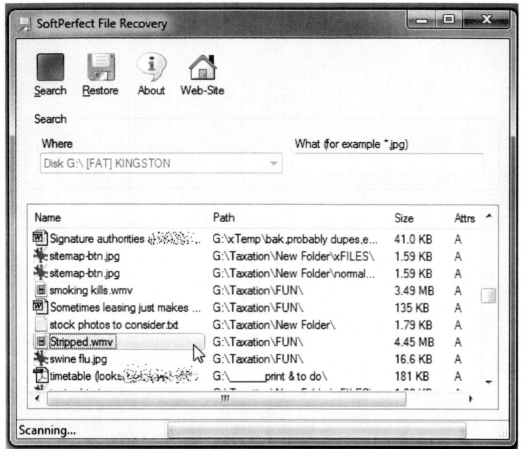

Figure: The previously deleted file STRIPPED.WMV is easily found and recovered

Now observe in the next series of screenshots as the relevant directory entry is ***purged*** using a recommended directory entry utility (see the 'Recommended Wiping Software' section on page 183). The utility's cluster examining tool finds the directory entry.

With a few clicks of the mouse, the directory entry is purged from the system.

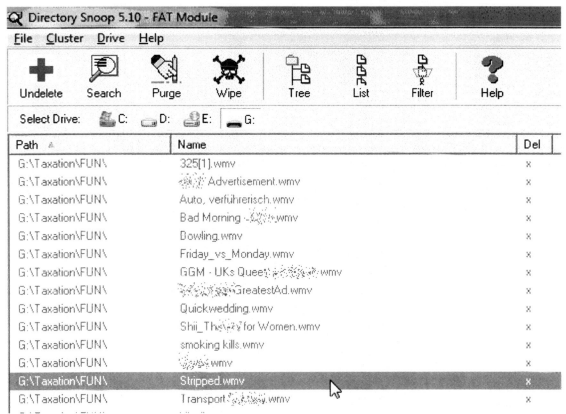

Figure: Disk drive analysis software easily locates the directory entry (i.e., the name of the old, deleted file)

Figure: Selecting the directory entry for purging and then confirming the purge

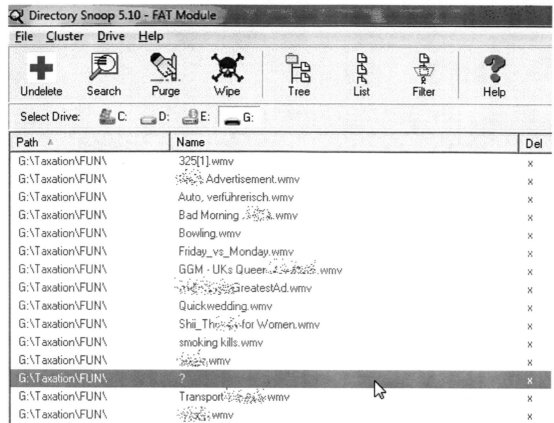

Figure: The directory entry is now purged and emptied from the disk's index, replaced with a ?

As you can see in the screenshot above, the name of the old, deleted file is now purged from the drive's FAT/NTFS index and the index entry is replaced with a question mark (?).

Now see if the undelete utility can find the old, deleted file by re-running the undelete utility. This is shown in the next screenshot.

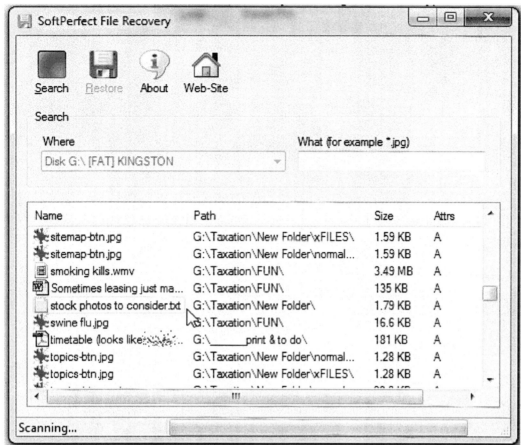

Figure: The undelete utility fails to find the STRIPPED.WMV file when you do another search

Even if you use the recovery utility to search for *all* deleted *.WMV file types on the USB stick, you will find no trace of the previous file as the directory entry is now gone. This is shown in the next screenshot.

As you can see in the screenshot above, the undelete utility can no longer find the record of the deleted file. This means that the deleted file is safe from being recovered with the undelete utility. However, until the drive's *fee space* is wiped, full-fledged forensic software probably could find and recover the file.

Therefore, for sensitive data, you should also wipe the drive's free space - as described in detail later in this chapter on page **Error! Bookmark not defined.** - to ensure that the data is beyond recovery even with expensive, full-fledged forensic software. This is because sophisticated forensic software is still able to recover data even when the relevant directory entries are purged from the drive index.

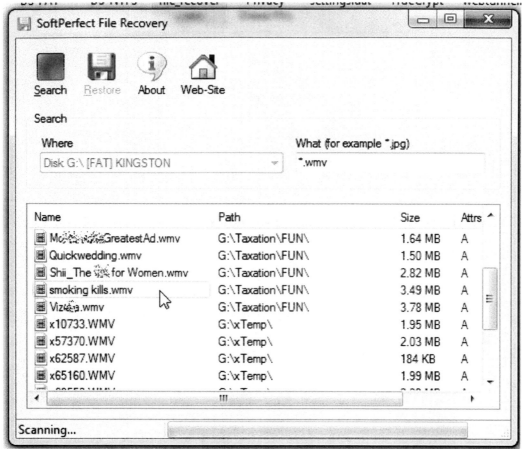

Figure: A comprehensive search of the entire drive reveals that the directory entry is purged

Purging All Your Directory Entries

Good data wiping software (see the section 'Recommended Wiping Software' on page 183) makes it easy to purge all empty directory entries from your system. This is shown in the next series of screenshots.

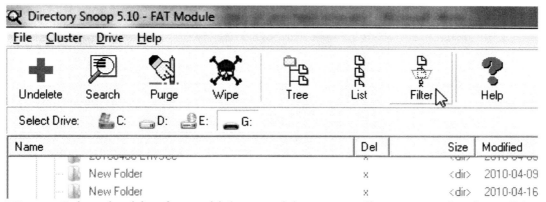

Figure: Select the drive from which you wish to purge directory entries (here G:)

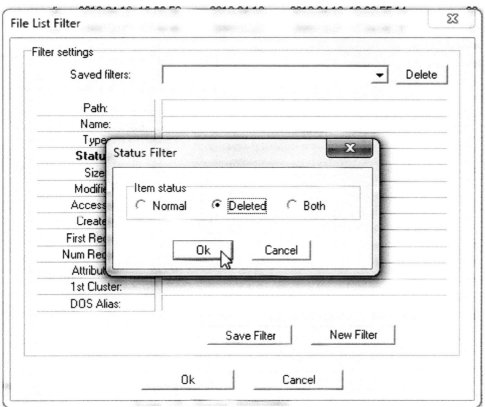

Figure: Filter the results to display the directory entries of previously deleted items

Figure: Press OK to apply the filter

Figure: The software now displays all directory entries for previously deleted items

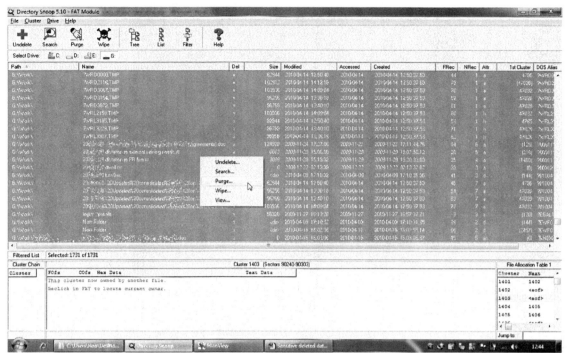

Figure: Select all the items you wish to purge, right-click on the selected items and choose
Purge...

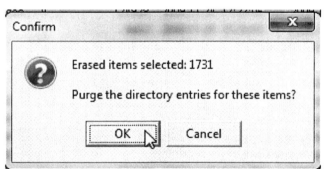

Figure: When you confirm the purge all the selected directory entries will be purged from
your system

After the mass purge of empty directory entrics from the USB stick you can now use a file
recovery (undelete) utility to confirm that no record remains of the old, deleted files or folders (i.e.,
that all the empty directory entries are in fact purged). This is shown in the next screenshot.

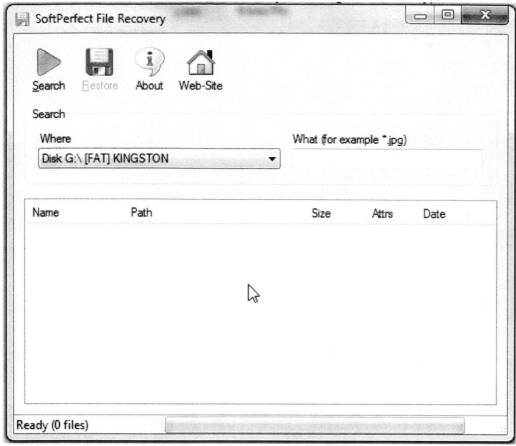

Figure: Confirm the purge was successful by re-running your file recovery (undelete) utility

Congratulations! All record and trace of names of old deleted files and folders have now been eliminated from the USB stick.

Of course, you can and should apply these same techniques to your hard drives (e.g., C: drive) in order to keep your entire system clear of this trace data.

Wiping Your Drive's Free Space

Now, it is all well and good that widely-available undelete utilities may not be able to find and recover your previously deleted files and folders. But, as previously mentioned, until the relevant drive's *fee space* is wiped, sophisticated forensic software probably could find and recover your deleted files and folders, even with the directory entries purged.

Therefore, you should then also take the extra step to *wipe the free space* on your storage media (whether your hard drives or, as in this chapter's example, a USB stick). This way, all traces of the former files and folders will be eliminated and beyond recovery.

The step of wiping the free space is shown in the next series of screenshots using the same recommended data wiping software (see page 183).

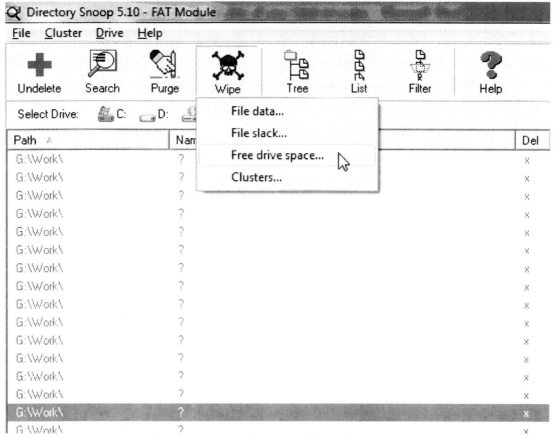

Figure: Now wipe the free space on the same drive that you have just purged of empty directory entries

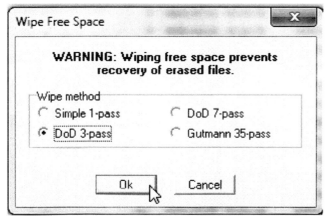

Figure: The more secure wiping method you use, the longer it will take

Once the wipe is complete, your deleted files and folders will be safely beyond recovery.

The Lessons Learned

To ensure that previously deleted data on your computer is beyond recovery, the lessons learned from the step-by-step demonstrations above are that you must:

- purge empty directory entries from your system (or at least those related to your sensitive files and folders that were deleted, moved, renamed and wiped) *and*

- wipe your drive's free space.

Chapter 15: Using Email, Webmail and Remailers

Introduction

Email and webmail remain as popular as ever. But if sent unencrypted, emails are an insecure means of communication. The best protection is through remailers, but these can be complicated. Depending on the sensitivity of your activities, you can also use webmail, or temporary and disposable email addresses.

This chapter will first explain the basics of email and show you why it is important to understand how email travels over the Internet; also, what email headers are all about. This chapter will explain that, at best, webmail accounts are semi-private, but easy to use, accessible with a browser and are also easy to cancel (or abandon) if spam gets out of control or if your identity is compromised.

The topic of temporary and disposable email accounts is covered and shows you that these are handy especially when you do not want to reveal your 'real' email account.

For more advanced users, remailers are introduced: these allow you to send an email in such a way that the recipient (or anyone intercepting the message intended for the recipient) will not be able to determine from where it came. Learn how to send emails (including with attachments) anonymously. Lastly, you will see that the best way to take advantage of remailers may be through easy-to-use web forms.

Email Basics

As a general rule, your sensitive activities should not be performed by ordinary email. Instead you should:

- **encrypt** your messages

- use a **webmail** account or, better yet, a reliable **remailer**

- access your account through a functioning **proxy** or **VPN** (recall see the 'Surfing Anonymously Using a Web Proxy' section on page 129), *and*

- **completely trust** the people with which you are corresponding, especially if the emails contain links or attachments

Understanding that Email Travels as Plain Text

Your email messages pass through several systems on their onward journey to the intended recipient(s). The system operator (or **administrator** or **sysop**) of each of those intermediary systems has the opportunity to read your messages as they pass through their system.

Therefore, unless you take special steps or use special software or services to encrypt your email messages, they travel in plain text over the Internet and are vulnerable to being saved, copied or read along their journey.

In addition, it is no secret that employers (in the US at least) routinely monitor employees' email messages. Employees should always assume that they have no privacy when sending emails using company equipment or facilities.

How Email Headers Give You Away

Every email consists of three elements:

1. memo-style information (i.e., To, From, Cc., Bcc., Date and Subject)
2. message body
3. headers

Depending on the software you use, you may never see the headers mentioned in #3 above, whereas all email software and services will typically display #1 and #2. While it is easy enough to change your email program's *From* setting (i.e., by putting in a fake email address), this is a low level of anonymity given the information contained in the *headers*.

Given the efforts to thwart spam, a number of tools and tutorials are available for tracking down the source of spammers by analyzing the headers in emails. However, these same tools can be used to track you down.

For example, if you do not take the basic steps detailed in this book to anonymize your email activities, a recipient can use the headers of your message and the InterNIC database to track down your service provider and complain to your email postmaster (i.e., possibly your employer). Or unscrupulous marketers or snoops could use your email and IP address to start building a profile about you. After all, experts warn that a mere 10 digits of information are needed to label uniquely each human being on the planet.

Key Email Headers Explained

Some fictional email headers are illustrated below. Most email software and webmail services do *not* display detailed header information by default. To see the detailed email headers, check for options such as 'Show all headers' or 'Show original' (for Gmail) in your software or webmail.

```
Return-Path: <from@anydomain.org>
X-SpamCatcher-Score: 1 [X]
Received: from [176.163.40.119] (HELO anydomain.org)
    by fe3.anydomain.org (CommuniGate Pro SMTP 4.1.8)
    with ESMTP-TLS id 61258719 for to@mail.anydomain.org;
Message-ID: <4129F3CA.2020509@anydomain.org>
Date: Wed, 21 Jan 2009 12:52:00 -0500 (EST)
From: Taylor Evans <from@anydomain.org>
User-Agent: Mozilla/5.0 (Windows; U; Windows NT 5.1; en-US; rv:1.0.1)
X-Accept-Language: en-us, en
MIME-Version: 1.0
To: Joe Blow <to@mail.anydomain.org>
Subject: Business Development Meeting
Content-Type: text/plain; charset=us-ascii; format=flowed
Content-Transfer-Encoding: 7bit
```

Figure: An example of some fictional email headers

> **From:** and **Reply-To:** (or **Reply-Path:** or **Return-Path:**)
> These basic 'memo-style' pieces of information are easily forged by modifying an email program's account Options. For example, from Microsoft Outlook Express' menu: **Tools > Accounts >** select account > **Properties** button > and change the *User Information* section to whatever *Name*, *Organization*, *Email address* and *Reply address* that you want.

> **Received:**
> This is the hardest header to forge and is thus the most reliable for tracking down the origins of an email. This header lists, in reverse chronological order, all the servers through which the message was relayed before reaching the recipient. Depending on the path taken by the email, some mail systems will add the IP address of the machine where the email originated.

> **Message-ID:**
> This is a unique value assigned to the message by the originating system that usually ends with the domain name of the machine from which the message was sent.

> **Comment:**
> Different software and mail systems may add additional information to the email's headers in the form of comments. An example of one revealing comment you sometimes see is that of *Authenticated sender*, the sender's supposed true identity.

Sender: (or **X-Sender:**)
>   This is another header you may sometimes see. Even if the "From:" header of an email is forged, the email software *may* (it's supposed to, but rarely does) insert the sender's true identity.

Testing Your Email for Privacy

To demonstrate the limitations of email privacy, check out an email testing service:

- http://www.emailfinder.com/

- http://www.ip-adress.com/trace_email/

- http://www.email-unlimited.com/tools/verify-email.aspx

- http://www.contactclean.com/lookup.php

- or type "reverse email trace" in your favorite search engine.

Webmail and Secure Mail Services

Introduction

Having a webmail account is a basic and rudimentary step towards your online privacy. You can usually sign up with a bare minimum of information. Accordingly, such accounts are easy to setup, including for a temporary purpose or to abandon later. There are also services offering temporary or disposable email addresses (see the next section, 'Temporary and Disposable Email Addresses').

Of course, your webmail account is only as secure as the passphrase you choose for it. Ensure that you use a strong passphrase that is difficult for novices to 'guess' and for hackers to 'crack' (see 'Chapter 3: Importance of Good Passwords and Passphrases' starting on page 23). However, having strong passphrases to access your emails is all well and good, but this won't prevent rogue system administrators (sysops) or opportune snoops from peeking at your messages. Only **encrypting** your communications will protect you against this risk.

Advantages of Webmail

Webmail also sometimes offers a form of security in that many reputable webmail providers use an **encrypted connection** (i.e., a Secure Sockets Layer or "SSL" connection) to protect email data while it is in transit. This is especially important if you are using a wireless network because 'normal' email (i.e., using an ordinary mail server like POP3) often means that the data is transmitted as plain text and can be more easily intercepted.

Another advantage of webmail accounts is that many include robust **spam filters** and virus scanning. With more and more providers providing essentially limitless storage, webmail is an ever increasingly attractive way of achieving a basic level of privacy and security.

The most secure webmail services include full encryption, not just the connection, but the message contents as well. Encryption helps to ensure that an email cannot be monitored, logged, analyzed and stored by your Internet service provider, your employer, or snoops who have or gain access to the messages.

Secure Mail Services

There are an endless number of potential webmail services for you to choose from. Because of this, a few services of particular interest are highlighted below. You can also type "private webmail accounts" or "encrypted webmail" into your favorite search engine.

When comparing any webmail services with your privacy and security in mind, pay attention to cookie dependence, message size, and proxy friendliness. Also read the provider's Terms of

Service and check their privacy policies especially regarding the disclosure of your personal data to third parties.

PrivacyHarbor.com
http://www.privacyharbor.com/

A well-respected, free secure email service.

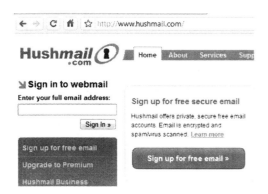

HushMail
http://www.hushmail.com/

HushMail has been in business since 1999, uses strong encryption and is considered a reliable secure email provider. Free accounts are available, but must be accessed frequently to remain active.

Anonymous Secure Email
https://www.anonymousspeech.com/

Features offshore servers, anonymity (no logging of IP addresses) and encryption. A free trial is available.

Setting up a Quasi-Anonymous Private Webmail Account

Remember that most webmail services log and may even track your IP address when you access or send mail via their service. This can be overcome by accessing the site while using a web proxy (see the 'Surfing Anonymously Using a Web Proxy' section on page 129).

Before signing up for your webmail account, make sure your proxy is working. See the 'Testing Your Proxy or VPN: What is My IP Address' section on page 141 for websites that tell you what your IP address is. Make sure that your browser is reporting the IP address of the proxy and not your real IP address. If your proxy is working, you are all set to sign up.

Configuration and set-ups vary between webmail services. Similarly, some services require *cookies* to work properly. If you must use a cookie-dependant webmail account, bypass this problem by temporarily choosing to accept cookies and once the cookie is in place, turn your cookies back off.

If the webmail service you want to access uses HTTP<u>S</u>, make sure that your proxy or VPN supports this, else visiting any such secure sites will normally by-pass your proxy or VPN and disclose your IP address (see the 'Testing Your Proxy or VPN: What is My IP Address?' section starting on page 141).

Tips when Signing Up

When signing-up for the webmail service, avoid as much as possible the disclosure of any personal information. Similarly, do not use any information that is personally identifiable as your "password hint."

Once signed up, continue to access your webmail account with your proxy or VPN enabled.

Don't Email, CC or BCC Your Personal Email Account

Another security tip is not to test your private webmail account by sending messages to your personal email address. There is no point going through all the trouble above as, should your private webmail become compromised, the hacker or adversary need only check your outbox. Similarly, never cc or bcc messages to your real email address.

Once your private webmail account is set up, you can use it for sending quasi-anonymous messages. You can send your webmail message to a remailer (see page 209) adding yet another layer of anonymity to your messages, if you wish. You can even post to newsgroups using webmail in conjunction with mail2news gateways (see 'Chapter 16: Usenet Newsgroups' for more details).

How to Use Your Private Webmail as Anonymously as Possible (Advanced Users)

Follow these guidelines to minimize your online footprint when using your private webmail account:

- use a proxy or VPN with your web browser (see the 'Surfing Anonymously Using a Web Proxy' section on page 129)

- make sure that the proxy or VPN is working by testing it at any number of testing sites (see the 'Always Test the Proxy' section on page 134)

- while using the now verified proxy or VPN, sign up for a private webmail account (see the 'Webmail and Secure Mail Services' section on page 203). If you need to verify the account with an already existing email address, use a temporary webmail account (see the 'Temporary and Disposable Email Addresses' section on page 207)

- always use the proxy or VPN when accessing your private webmail account (including sending messages and even when only reading your messages). Remember that logs of requesting IP addresses are probably being kept by the webmail provider. Similarly, never CC or BCC your 'real' email address

- consider only using your private webmail account when a reply is needed, otherwise access a web-based remailer while using a proxy to send anonymous messages or mail2news Usenet posts (see the sections 'Web-based Anonymous Remailers' and 'Posting Anonymously to Usenet (Advanced Users)' on pages 213 and 237, respectively)

- if you are truly paranoid and have accessed the webmail account without a proxy or VPN enabled, abandon the account, never access it again, start over and set up a new private webmail account

Temporary and Disposable Email Addresses

Introduction

These services can be quite handy. They allow you to have a temporary email address for any sensitive activity for which you do not wish to disclose your 'real' email address, like when signing up for an on-line service. This can also help you to avoid being placed on **spam lists**.

Disposable email addresses are especially handy if you only intend to use an email address *once*. For example, often when you sign up to take a look at a new service (e.g., a dating website) you are sent a confirmation email to which you have to reply in order to activate the service. Instead of using your 'real' email address (which could be added to spam lists) use a temporary email address for the confirmation step. Once your account on the new website is set up, the temporary email address can then safely expire because you no longer need it. This way, you have kept your 'real' email address private and away from potential spam mailing lists or other abuse.

Some Services to Try

Mail Expire - http://www.mailexpire.com/ - allows you to easily create an email alias and set the amount of time before it expires (from 12 hours to months). Unfortunately, the aliases it provides are not that pleasing to the eye (e.g., tlaingeica@ farifluset.mailexpire.com) so the service may be better suited for automatic sign-ups rather than for providing to real people.

Guerrilla Mail - http://www.guerrillamail.com/ - provides email addresses that last 15 minutes and which you can use to read and reply to emails in this time.

Mailinator - http://mailinator.com/ - allows users to create an on-the-spot email identity that provides anonymity in one easy step and has alternate domains.

My Trash Mail - http://mytrashmail.com/ - temporary email addresses for 2 to 3 hours (and longer periods with a paid version of the service).

SneakMail - http://sneakemail.com/ - less user-friendly but still good, as it also lets you reply to emails.

Anonymous Contact - http://www.anonymouscontact.com/ - slightly different, this service forwards email between two communicating parties, back and forth, and never reveals the email addresses of either party.

More About: Self-destructing communications

Self-destructing communications are similar to temporary and disposable emails as these services allow you to send email communications with an expiry date.

self-destructing email - http://www.self-destructing-email.com/ - free trial available

KickNotes - http://www.kicknotes.com/

privnote - https://privnote.com/

Introduction to Remailers

The Basics

A **remailer** is a process that makes your email messages anonymous. Some services also let you post anonymously to Usenet newsgroups through so-called mail2news gateways (see 'Chapter 16: Usenet Newsgroups' for more details). By using a remailer, you can send messages without the recipient(s) ever knowing from whom it came. The process works like this:

- you send your message to the remailer (by regular email or webmail) using some special syntax

- the remailer "strips away" all of the header information (recall the 'Key Email Headers Explained' section on page 201) such as name and reply-to address that indicate the origin of the message

- the remailer then forwards your anonymized message to the intended recipient

---

Top Tip

Because remailing can be a complicated process, consider using a web-based remailer which is easier and more convenient (see the next section, 'Web-based Anonymous Remailers', on page 213).

To make messages even more anonymous, it is sometimes possible to **chain** remailers by sending a message through two or more remailers. While chaining does increase anonymity, the more remailers in a chain, the more likely your message may never reach the intended recipient. This is for a variety of reasons:

- remailers are primarily operated by privacy hobbyists for free and thus reliability varies among providers

- remailers are subject to abuse by spammers which may hurt their performance

- system downtimes occur similar to any other computer-based service

Remailers are changing all the time so you should always first check the relevant website or the Usenet newsgroup **alt.privacy** for all of the latest information on remailers. If you do not know what a newsgroup is or how to access one, please see 'Chapter 16: Usenet Newsgroups' starting on page 217. In addition, you should always send an email to the remailer with the subject "remailer-help" to obtain its most recent help file and instructions on how to properly use the service.

At the time of writing, here are some addresses you can try:

mixmaster@remailer.privacy.at   remailer@rip.ax.lt
remailer@kroken.dynalias.com   hsub@mixmaster.mixmin.net
remailer@reece.net.au   remailer@dizum.com

or consult the remailer statistics at http://www.noreply.org/echolot/ or http://pinger.mixmin.net/

or type "reliable remailers" in your favorite search engine

Some remailers will even let you delay the time between when the remailer receives your email and forwards it onwards to your intended recipient. This prevents someone from analyzing Internet traffic and implicating you as the sender by determining that you had sent the message to a remailer just before the intended recipient received an email from a remailer.

The remailer's instructions will indicate whether the ability to delay the forwarding of messages (sometimes called "latency") is supported.

Remailer 'Syntax'

You can send your message to a remailer using your own email or webmail account. Webmail is of course preferred as you can access it with a proxy or VPN for additional security and privacy.

The instructions and syntax for using remailers can be somewhat complicated:

- the **To:** field of your outgoing message should be addressed to a remailer since the message must first be redirected through a remailer.

- the **Subject**: field of your outgoing message will be irrelevant as the remailer will delete it when stripping the headers from your message, but fill it in anyway [e.g., "Anonymous" (no quotes)].

- no matter which remailer you use, the **body** of your message MUST be in the format below. It is **imperative** that your first line begin with 2 colons.

```
::
Request-Remailing-To: [email address of your intended recipient]
[blank line]
##
Subject: [this will appear as the Subject of your message]
[any additional header commands - if not, omit this line]
[blank line]
[start the text of your message on this line]
```

How Private is Private?

Because you are relying on a third party for remailing, the privacy of your messages and identity is only as good as the integrity of the remailer operator. Remember, the message arrives at the remailer as a normal email message with your identity intact. Theoretically, risks might include:

- the remailer operator reading your forwarded mail (and who knows who they are or who they work for?)

- it may still be possible for an adversary to compel the remailer operator to reveal your identity (e.g., through extortion or a court order)

- a snoop or hacker could covertly break in and monitor the remailer

Mixmaster Remailers

In response to these concerns with "classic remailers" above (called Cypherpunk or Type I remailers), second generation remailers have emerged which incorporate chaining *and* encryption technology.

The newer generation of anonymous remailers is called Mixmaster or Type II remailers. These types of remailers also employ encryption to maximize privacy. Each Mixmaster remailer will have a public encryption key you'll need to use. Messages make two or more stops along their journey in order that no one service knows the identity of both the sender and recipient. Mixmaster-type remailers enhance security further by parsing all messages into equal-sized packets that are only reassembled at the final remailer before being forwarded to the intended recipient.

If a remailer supports these Mixmaster features its email address will often start with mixmaster@. But in any event, whether Mixmaster features are supported will be clearly spelled out in the remailer's most recent help file.

Remailers and Attachments

Because remailers are the most secure means of transmitting Internet messages, they may appeal to you. Even if you do send attachments via remailers do so selectively and first make sure that the remailer supports the transmission of attachments.

In any event, most remailers will have a maximum file size and you may have to first encode the file (see the next 'More About' box) which may further limit your ability to send a multitude of attachments via remailers.

More About: Encoding and Decoding

Encoding and decoding refer to the conversion of binary files (e.g., images or videos) into plain text (ASCII characters). Most applications do encoding automatically or in the background. But sometimes for remailers (and email or Usenet) you may have to manually encode or decode files.

As email and Usenet can only handle text, encoding is the process whereby binary files are translated into text. When you receive the text message it is necessary for you to translate it back to a binary file (i.e., decoding). When you want to send or post a file, it is necessary for you to first translate it into text (i.e., encoding). If you download an email or Usenet message that contains garbled characters it could be that the message is an encoded file that you need to decode.

The most popular encoding and decoding methods are *UU* and *yEnc*. Different utilities are available for each of these methods which are easy to find with your favorite search engine.

Web-based Anonymous Remailers

Introduction

As mentioned in the previous section, a remailer helps make your email messages anonymous (and sometimes Usenet posts also). By using a remailer, you can send messages that do not reveal you as the source.

Remailers can be quite complicated and technical, but some web-based remailers make the process much easier. The information you enter into the web-based form is formatted seamlessly in the background for proper syntax and then forwarded to a remailer. As always to maximize anonymity, you should access the remailer web form through a proxy or VPN (see 'Chapter 11: Protecting Your Identity and IP Address with Anonymous Surfing' starting on page 121).

Top Tip

Although web-based remailers are easier to use, these services may not provide the same high level of anonymity as the remailers described in the previous section. As with any intermediary type service (like proxy services), you should always carefully assess the integrity of any web-based anonymous remailer you wish to use.

Some Web-based Remailers You Can Try

Given the nature of these services, they can come and go at times. You can also type *"anonymous web remailer"* in your favorite search engine, but be prepared to dig and to heed the tip above about doing your homework.

Some web-based remailers are presented below.

StayIncognito

http://www.stayincognito.com/email.php

A straight-forward and easy-to-use interface.

AnonEmail (via Anonymouse.org)

http://anonymouse.org/anonemail.html

Anonymouse has been around for over 10 years in support of Internet anonymity.

Global Internet Liberty Campaign W3 Anonymous Remailer

http://gilc.org/speech/anonymous/remailer.html

Another simple interface that has been around for years.

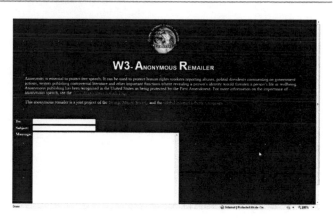

Chapter 16: Usenet Newsgroups

Introduction

Usenet newsgroups, though often overlooked, are a great source of downloads and information. In this chapter, you will learn what Usenet newsgroups are all about. You will also come to understand the privacy risks of Usenet newsgroups, especially if you post messages. The unbiased collection of Usenet newsgroup software and tools presented in this chapter will help you on your way.

You will learn that many Internet service providers (ISP) limit access to certain newsgroups, especially the 'binary' groups and you will be shown how to use open servers and access newsgroups that your ISP may have banned or censored. If you do not mind paying a little extra, this chapter includes an unbiased listing of commercial, sometimes called 'premium', Usenet service providers.

Finally, if you wish to contribute (post) to Usenet newsgroups, you will learn how to post messages as anonymously as possible to protect your identity and privacy.

About Usenet (and its many Downloads)

The Basics

Usenet is a collection of Internet newsgroups and is simply another standalone 'element' of the Internet, just like the World Wide Web, email and chatting. Usenet's structure is completely decentralized and still represents somewhat of an untamed frontier. It is akin to a huge database that is continually on the move between the thousands of various computer servers hosting its contents (a mass of newsgroup messages). If your ISP can offer you Usenet access, your ISP either hosts the Usenet database on its own servers or, more likely these days, uses a large, specialist third-party Usenet provider.

Like the other elements of the Internet, Usenet requires its own software (called a **newsreader**) and has its own terminology and structure. When accessing Usenet with newsreader software, think of the process like email except that the Inbox and its messages are open to everyone for reading (downloading) and sending (uploading or posting), and that there are thousands of Inboxes, one for every conceivable topic of interest.

Like email, people can post messages to newsgroups that include attachments (called **binaries**). Many newsgroups specialize in binaries, especially video, picture, music and other media files. There are tens of thousands of newsgroups available on the Internet in total and there is a binary sub-group for every topic of interest. However, it is important to remember that the number and type of available newsgroups will vary from ISP to ISP.

How Usenet is Organized

Newsgroups are organized in a hierarchy. Similar to domain names (e.g., www.example.com), the component names of a newsgroup are separated by dots. The first segment of the name is the main way newsgroups are categorized.

The "big eight" categories of the Usenet hierarchy (the 'normal' and non-binary newsgroups) are as follows:

Name	Category	Name	Category
COMP.*	computers	REC.*	Recreation
HUMANITIES.*	humanities	SCI.*	Science
MISC.*	miscellaneous	SOC.*	Society
NEWS.*	news	TALK.*	Talk

However, you may not be as interested in the big eight as you are in the `alt.` hierarchy which stands for "<u>alt</u>ernative." Many users are specifically interested in the `alt.binaries.*` newsgroups.

Many ISPs do not carry some or even many of the newsgroups, especially the *binary newsgroups*. Depending on your ISP, you may have access to none or hundreds of these binary sub-groups. Because some can be controversial, many ISPs will carry only a subset of what is fully available, essentially "censoring" the rest.

What Are You Missing? (Censored Newsgroups)

To compare what your current ISP carries to what is potentially available, full newsgroup listings and newsgroup searches are available in a number of places (usually from commercial Usenet providers). You can try:

- full newsgroup search at http://www.giganews.com/performance.html#ng-search

- full newsgroup search at http://www.usenetserver.com/en/searchgroups.php

- list of newsgroups at http://www.easynews.com/groups.list

- yet another list of newsgroups at http://www.easynews.com/list-all-groups.phtml

- or type "full newsgroup listing" in your favorite search engine

Access to Usenet newsgroups may be part of your Internet account package. If you do not have access to the groups you would like, you can try to access so-called **open servers** (news servers available for the general public to use). Another option is to pay separately for access to Usenet newsgroups through a specialized commercial service, sometimes referred to as a **premium Usenet server**. Both of these options - open servers and premium Usenet providers - are addressed later in this chapter.

What is Newsreader Software?

Just as you need a browser for web surfing, an email client for sending/receiving email and an IRC client for Internet chatting, you will require **newsreader** software for retrieving and posting messages from and to Usenet. Rather than using any built-in features of your operating system (e.g., Outlook Express for Windows), it is recommended that you use a stand-alone newsreader, for much the same reasons that you should also use a separate, stand-alone web browser for sensitive activities (see the 'Using a Separate Web Browser for Sensitive Activities' section on page 143).

Like email software, you will need to enter some basic information into your newsreader including a special Internet address of the news server from where it can download a list of available newsgroups (often, `news.example.com`). The protocol used by Usenet's news servers and your newsreader software is called Network News Transfer Protocol or **NNTP** for short.

An example of these settings is shown in the next screenshot.

Figure: Entering a news server address in your newsreader software

Most newsreaders also ask or allow you to enter personal information like your name and email address (see the next screenshot). To protect your privacy, do not use your real name and email address or any other personal data. Either leave these blank or enter aliases. Why? Because spammers are notorious for harvesting email addresses and other personal information from Usenet.

Figure: Do *not* enter any personally identifiable information in your newsreader settings

When you first connect to a news server, your newsreader software will download all of the available newsgroups from your ISP. From this list you choose the groups you want to **subscribe**. Most newsreaders will allow you to search for newsgroups by keyword. This lets you quickly find and subscribe to groups that represent the topics that you are most interested in (e.g., the binaries newsgroups).

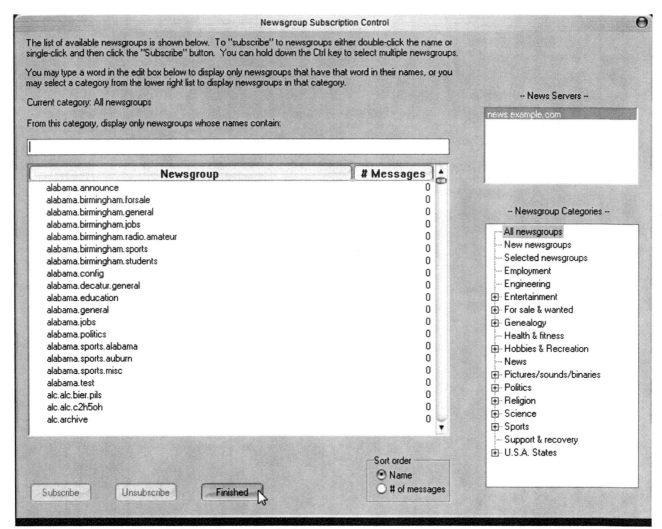

Figure: The newsreader displays the available groups you can subscribe to and often allows you to search the names of newsgroups

---

! Warning !

Please read all of 'Chapter 16: Usenet Newsgroups' before attempting to **post** to Usenet newsgroups.

What People Can Find Out About Your Usenet Newsgroup Activities

When you post to Usenet or even only retrieve messages, there are a number of risks you must understand.

Posting is Traceable

First, the entire Usenet from its inception has been and continues to be archived (for example, see Google's Groups (http://groups.google.com/advanced_search) which contains 20+ years' worth of Usenet archives! This means that unless you have given anonymity some thought, any and all posts you make (attaching files or otherwise) will be recorded. Such posts could come back to haunt you. Imagine a potential employer who routinely searches applicants' names in the Usenet records contained in Google Group's database as part of its candidate screening process.

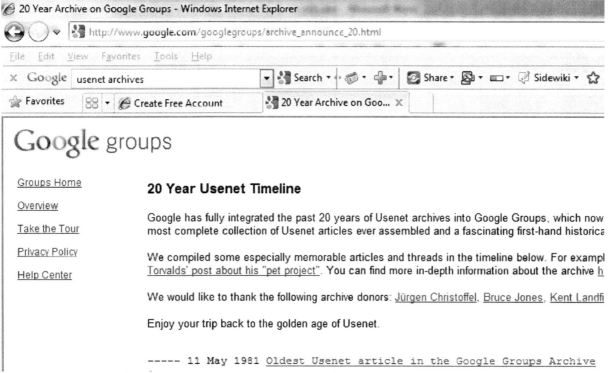

Figure: Decades of Usenet messages have been archived, so be careful what you post

To illustrate the privacy risks of posting to Usenet, browse any Google Groups message at http://groups.google.com/ or use the **Advanced Groups Search** to find a message of interest. Once you have opened a message, click on ***More options*** and then ***Show original***. Notice how some of the fields contain potentially revealing information (such as the message ID or even an IP address)! When you post to Usenet newsgroups without taking measures to protect your privacy, revealing details may be passed on in the posts and, once posted, may be impossible to undo.

At an absolute minimum, you should not enter your name and return email address in the Settings of your newsreader software. But even though this makes your posts untraceable for simple Google-type searches, there are still more precautions you should take.

"Fake" Posting is Still Traceable

Even if you post to Usenet using an alias or fake name and email address, the post is still traceable back to you. Just as your Internet browsing patterns and email messages can be traced back to you, so too can Usenet posts. Like email (recall the 'How Email Headers Give You Away' materials at page 200), Usenet posts contain a number of **headers**. Through one or more of these headers, the originating IP address can be determined which, in combination with other resources such as your ISP's logs or a profiler's records, could result in a breach of your privacy.

For example, the following headers may be traceable: MESSAGE-ID (shown in the next screenshot), NNTP POSTING HOST LINE and PATH LINE.

```
From: mtbai...@sonetis.com (Matthew Bailey)
Subject: !NAMTAR!.WAD Homepage is on-line.  Screenshots,
demos and the WAD itself all available now.
Date: 1996/05/28
Message-ID: <4o2dq8$hs4@lisa.iosphere.net>#1/1
X-Deja-AN: 157150554
sender: t...@mantis.co.uk
content-type: text/plain; charset=iso-8859-1
organization: Channel One
mime-version: 1.0
reply-to: mtbai...@sonetis.com
newsgroups: rec.games.computer.doom.announce
```

Figure: Usenet posts contain a number of headers, some of which you may not even be aware of

The vast majority of ISPs log their news server activities. The logs are primarily used to deal with complaints. By comparing the headers of a post to the ISP's log, the person who posted the message can be determined notwithstanding that they did so using an alias or a fake name and email address.

To post **anonymously**, you need to do so through a news server that omits any traceable path back to you. Even when you find a server that eliminates traceable headers, ALWAYS do a test post to the **alt.test** newsgroup to ensure the NNTP posting host line does *not* appear or that it has been altered to show a different IP address than yours (some news servers may replace the line with their own IP address).

Even Only "Lurking" Leaves a Trail

If you only read and download messages and never post (sometimes called **lurking**), even these activities might be logged by your ISP, including for legal reasons.

Conventional wisdom is that your ISP simply does not have the time or resources to scan through the logs to discover from which newsgroups and the individual posts their users are downloading. However, you should still be aware of this. You may want to check your ISP's *privacy policies* in respect of whether they are logging, what they log and how long they keep logs.

The safest way even to lurk may be to access newsgroups through an open public news sever (see the next section) or via a reliable commercial Usenet service that limits logging (see the 'Commercial Usenet Services' section on page 230).

Don't Confuse Achieving Usenet Anonymity with Using a Web Proxy

As already mentioned, just as email uses the SMTP protocol and web browsing uses the HTTP protocol, newsreader software uses the **NNTP protocol**. Note that the techniques you can use to become anonymous on the web will *not* make you anonymous for newsgroup postings.

Therefore, the techniques you learned in 'Chapter 11: Protecting Your Identity and IP Address with Anonymous Surfing' about using a proxy or VPN to mask your identity on the web will *not* work in the same way for your Usenet newsreader. A proxy or VPN masks the HTTP protocol activity whereas your newsreader uses the NNTP protocol which the web proxy or VPN service will *not* mask.

A web proxy or VPN service will only work if you are using a web-based Usenet service of which they are a few. In this case alone, the proxy or VPN will prevent your true IP address from being revealed and passed along by the web-based service.

Please also note that posting to newsgroups through a commercial service is not necessarily anonymous either.

Accessing Open News Servers

As mentioned in the 'About Usenet (and its many Downloads)' section, your ISP probably censors your access to some or certain newsgroups, especially in the **alt.binaries.*** hierarchy.

There are three main ways to access newsgroups that your ISP does not carry:

1. Using open news servers that are listed on the web (discussed below)

2. Using third party commercial services (see the 'Commercial Usenet Services' section on page 230)

3. For advanced users, using NNTP "sniffer" software (see the 'Accessing Open News Servers with an NNTP Sniffer (Advanced Users)' section on page 226)

More About: Open News Servers

As its name suggests, an *open news server* is a news server freely accessible by the public. Usually, you have to pay for access to Usenet newsgroups through a news server operated by your ISP or a separate Usenet provider. Open news servers can be accessed freely without charge; as a result, they usually have a very limited number of newsgroups available. Open news servers are frequently operated by educational institutions or Usenet enthusiasts.

Open News Servers Listed on the Web

Below are a number of links to websites that list open news servers. Many links of this nature come and go. If you are getting dead links when clicking on them, keep drilling down the list or type "open news servers" in your favorite search engine.

Please note that access to open news servers may also vary from ISP to ISP. This means that you may be able to access a particular open news server, but your friend who uses a different ISP may not. The reasons for this are quite technical and not covered here.

newzbot Public News Servers
http://www.newzbot.com/

> A list of open servers ranked (and sortable by) the number of groups carried, server speed, message count or the length of time it has been open to the public. The service also allows you to search for a particular newsgroup at http://www.newzbot.com/search.php.

Disenter
http://www.disenter.com/
> Search Usenet newsgroups that have been combined from dozens of open news servers, including binary newsgroups.

Publicly Accessible Free Usenet News Servers
http://freenews.maxbaud.net/
> This comprehensive and up-to-date site allows you to search for specific newsgroups.

Public News Server Web Ring
http://www.webring.com/hub?ring=nntp
> A list of participating Public News Server sites.

Open Directory Project (dmoz) List of Open Public News Servers
http://www.dmoz.org/Computers/Usenet/Public_News_Servers/
> A list of open news server sites.

Using the Open News Server Settings

To first test and then use any of the open servers listed at these sites, change your newsreader's **News Server** setting in your software's Settings, Options or Preferences and then look for *News Server* or *NNTP*. Type in the specific NNTP address in the *News Server:* box. See some sample screenshots below.

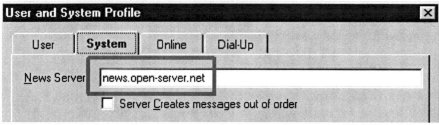

Figure: Look for a place to enter the News Server or NNTP address in your newsreader software's Settings, Options or Preferences

News Server & Authentication Information

You must enter the name of your news (nntp) host. You may need to contact your ISP for this information.

The hostname usually looks something like "news.ispname.com", where ispname is the name of your internet service provider. If all else fails, you can usually find an existing working news program on your machine (assuming you have one) and get the host name from it.

NNTP host names are also sometimes referred to as 'news server names', 'news host names' , or 'usenet server names'.

News (nntp) host

news.server.com

Authentication

User Name:

Password:

Misc Options

☑ Always send authinfo at log-on

☐ Use secure / encrypted connection (SSL)

☐ Enable SPA (Experimental!)

Ok   Cancel   Help

Figure: The News Server (NNTP) settings in a different newsreader

You can now subscribe, retrieve and view attachments for the listed groups as if you were connected to your ISP's news server. Using an open server may sometimes be slower but gives you access to more groups than before, and *generally* increases your privacy. You may even be able to *post* Usenet messages through some open news servers.

Top Tip

Never post through an open server unless you are certain that your IP address will not appear in any of the message headers. The only way to be sure is to post a test message, then retrieve it and look at the headers. The appropriate newsgroup for doing this is the **alt.test** group. Please follow proper Usenet etiquette and insert the word "ignore" (no quotes) in the post's subject line.

The anonymizing character of any open server can come and go - depending on abuse by spammers and a number of other factors - so always first conduct a test before posting to ensure that your IP address is not appearing in the message headers.

Recommended Usenet Software

Below is a list of Usenet software and utilities recommended at the time of writing.

Newsreader Software

GrabIt (by Shemes) - freeware - http://www.shemes.com/

> GrabIt may take some time to get used to, but after fiddling around with it for about an hour you should understand it well. **SBNews** (http://www.sb-software.com/sbnews/) is also a potentially suitable choice, but if you have a DSL cable and want to grab the binaries from a number of newsgroups, you will be downloading massive amounts of data, most of which you might not use. This is where GrabIt is so handy. GrabIt allows you to preview articles and is good about letting you know which multiple part files (i.e., big media files usually) are complete or not. This saves you from wasting time and bandwidth downloading incomplete posts. The downloading is also handy because GrabIt presents them in a 'batch' window. You can increase or decrease the priority of a specific download, pause all your downloads, or have your computer automatically shut down after the download batch is complete. After investing a little bit of time getting to know it, GrabIt is a good choice. Plus it is free.

Agent (by Forte) - about $30 - http://www.forteinc.com/agent/

> Agent is a good, standard newsreader, but only free for a trial period. It is a popular newsreader for downloading posts and extracting files from Usenet messages together with powerful built-in watch and kill filter capabilities. There used to be a free version ("Free Agent") but alas no longer.

NNTP Utilities

News Hunter 4 (by Jonathan Zarate) - freeware - it can be difficult to find so type "News Hunter 4" in your favorite search engine or torrent search

> This NNTP sniffer helps you find open (public) news servers to enable you to access newsgroups your ISP may be censoring (see the 'What Are You Missing? (Censored Newsgroups)' section on page 218).

Commercial Usenet Services

Introduction

Another way to obtain fuller access to Usenet newsgroups is to pay for it. The services listed below are not free, but the quality is good and usually marked by long *retention periods* (meaning older posts stay available for download longer), fast downloading and the largest number of available newsgroups, including the binaries groups.

Each service provider will have its own set-up instructions and, once you have signed up with them, *NNTP-based services* will provide you with the news server host address to enter into your newsreader software. *Web-based services* allow you to access Usenet newsgroups through your web browser; you will normally not need a news server host address for a web-based service, but will need a username and password.

Usenet Services

Below is a list of third-party commercial Usenet services, sometimes referred to as "premium news servers," that you may wish to consider.

NNTP-Based Services

SecureTunnel
https://www.securetunnel.com/personal/encrypted-usenet

SecureTunnel offers a reasonably priced *encrypted* Usenet service. User experience with the support team has been good.

Giganews
http://www.giganews.com/

Giganews' website includes a full newsgroup search at http://www.giganews.com/performance.html#ng-search so you can see if they carry the newsgroups that you want.

UseNetServer
http://www.usenetserver.com/en

UseNetServer offers its current group list for your perusal at http://www.usenetserver.com/groups.txt and a newsgroup search at http://www.usenetserver.com/en/searchgroups.php.

Web-Based Services

EasyNews
http://www.easynews.com/

> EasyNews uses a handy *web-based* interface, has high retention rates and seems to boast an aggressive privacy policy. You can see a full list of the groups available on its news servers at http://www.easynews.com/list-all-groups.phtml.

NewsGuy
http://www.newsguy.com/

> A long-standing, *web-based* Usenet provider. NewsGuy offers a free, 14-day trial and uses encrypted SSL connections.

Accessing Open News Servers with an NNTP Sniffer (Advanced Users)

As mentioned in the 'About Usenet (and its many Downloads)' section starting on page 217, your ISP probably censors some newsgroups, especially in the `alt.binaries.*` hierarchy. One way to gain access to these groups is to find an open news server (i.e., a news server open to the public) carrying them.

In addition to the listing of open news servers found on the Internet (some are provided in the 'Accessing Open News Servers' section on page 226), another way to locate open news servers is to use NNTP "**sniffer**" software. This NNTP sniffing is essentially what the operators of those websites do in order to find and then list open news servers.

Using NNTP Sniffer Software

NNTP sniffer software helps you track down open news servers. Because you perform the search yourself, this method has the advantage of finding open news servers that are accessible from your particular ISP. Recall from the 'Accessing Open News Servers' section on page 226, that access to open news servers may vary from ISP to ISP.

NNTP sniffer software basically uses your own ISP as a starting point and tries to find as many other news servers as it can. Then, the software tests each one in turn to see which is an open server (i.e., open to the public).

The software usually needs to start with an NNTP server and newsgroup. You can enter your current ISP's news service (e.g., *news*.example.com) and the `alt.test` newsgroup, or some other newsgroup that you know your ISP carries.

From there the software will do the rest and present you with a list of available open news servers and the groups that they carry. Depending on the functionality of the software, it may also tell you which servers allow posting as well as the speed and the latency of posts (latency means how long posts are available).

! Warning !

Some ISPs consider the use of NNTP sniffer software as an undesirable activity (some may even liken it to "hacking") so please first *carefully* read your ISP's Terms of Service to make sure you are not prohibited from using sniffer software. Do *not* try using NNTP sniffer software if you have *any* doubts after reading your ISP's Terms of Service.

Some sample screenshots are presented below (with server names blurred out), but appearances will vary for different NNTP sniffer software.

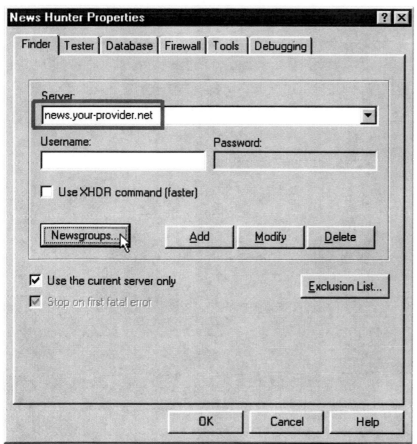

Figure: You will need to enter a starting NNTP news server address

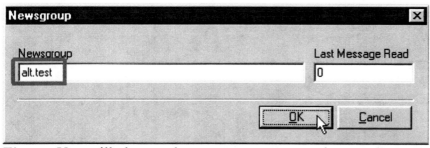

Figure: You will also need to enter a newsgroup that you know the news server carries

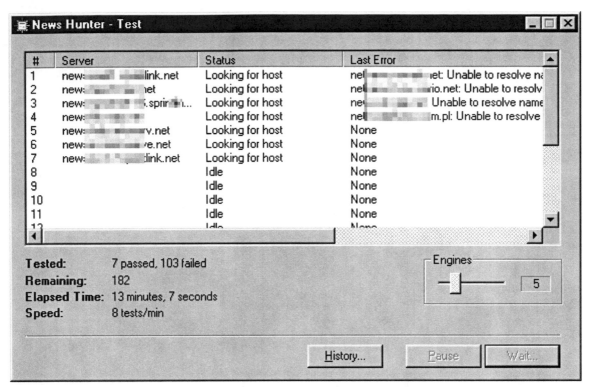

Figure: The sniffer software will start to probe news servers to determine whether they are 'open' to the public or not

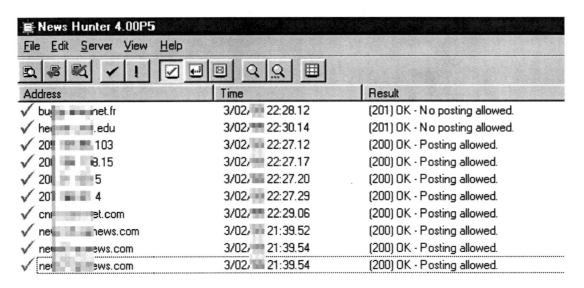

Figure: When the sniffer software is finished, it will present a list of available open news servers

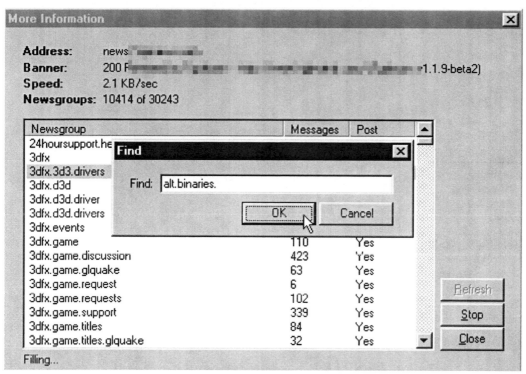

Figure: Once the sniffer software finds open news servers it will let you browse and search among the available newsgroups

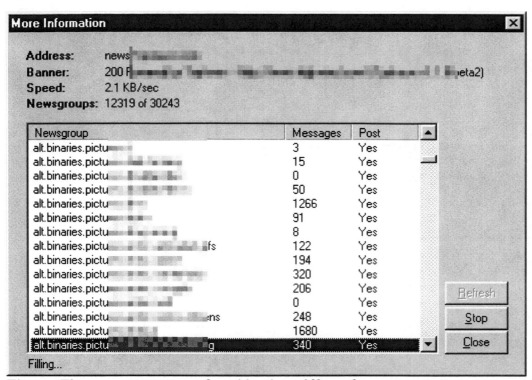

Figure: The open news server found by the sniffer software seems to carry many binaries groups

Posting Anonymously to Usenet (Advanced Users)

Introduction

As previously outlined, Usenet is the oldest Internet-based bulletin board discussion system. The network is still much in use, despite the rise of web forums and social networking sites. The unique difference between Usenet and web-based forums is that Usenet is not maintained on a single centralized server or server farm. The newsgroups that comprise Usenet are scattered all over a constantly changing group of servers that store and forward messages to each other as news feeds.

The Risks of Posting to Usenet

All messages you send to Usenet contain information that could identify you, such as your IP address in the technical (usually hidden) information that is sent as headers along with your message. These headers are somewhat similar to those for emails that were discussed in the 'How Email Headers Give You Away' section on page 200. The headers may vary depending on how and where you're logged in from. Below is a fictional sample of a header (the bolded lines indicate those that contain information that could potentially identify the person who posted the message):

Newsgroups: soc.support.fat-acceptance,atl.general, mindspring.local.atlanta
Path: mindspring!firehose.mindspring.com!newsfeed1-hme1!
        newsfeed.internetmci.com!128.174.5.49!vixen.cso.uiuc.edu!
        uchinews!news
From: Suzy Smith <user@uiuc.edu>
Subject: Re: Help with headers?
Nntp-Posting-Host: ip14.an4-atlanta2.ga.pub-ip.psi.net
Message-ID: <32146bef.20423023@news.interamp.com>
Reply-To: suzy@other.place
Organization: Anything You Like
References: <20110901140100.KAA29407@ladder02.news.aol.com>
        <EFy5Ar.3pq@world.std.com><340DC46C.3A62@wco.com>
        <5umekl$44m@dfw-ixnews9.ix.netcom.com> <5v3g50hsl1@news.smart.net>
Date: Tue, 9 Sep 2011 21:17:39 GMT
X-Newsreader: AOL Offline Reader
X-No-Archive: yes
Lines: 24

You may wish to post anonymously to a Usenet newsgroup. The reasons may vary - due to general privacy concerns, or if you wish to cloak your identity from current or potential employers, or to prevent spammers from acquiring your email address, or to ensure hackers do not try to target your system and so on.

This section describes the various ways you may post anonymously to Usenet newsgroups. Please remember that it is *not* enough to type in a 'fake' name and email address into the required fields of your newsreader's configuration settings - your news server will still insert enough information in your newsgroup posts that could identify the source and make the message potentially traceable back to you.

Please note that in most cases these methods require your absolute trust in a third party (i.e., that the operator of the service is not reading, copying or monitoring messages before anonymizing and forwarding them).

! Warning !

Trying to post anonymously to Usenet using the methods below is truly for *advanced users* only. It is not an easy process; make a mistake and your IP address could be revealed undermining the whole point of you trying to post anonymously.

Method 1: Using a Web-based Remailer

The first way to post anonymously is to use one of the widely available anonymous remailer services along with a mail2news gateway. This is a two-step process.

Step 1 of 2

Send your intended post using a web-based remailer service such as AnonEmail (http://anonymouse.org/anonemail.html). Other web-based remailers can be found in the section 'Web-based Anonymous Remailers' on page 213.

Basically, the remailer service will receive your message, strip out all the original header information, including your IP address, and then re-send the message to its final destination, with its own new headers attached. This ensures that you are not identified as the original source of the message.

Ideally, the web-based remailer service should support an encrypted SSL connection (i.e., https://), but these are hard to find.

The major drawback with this method is that you must have absolute faith in the web-based remailer - that the service is indeed doing what they claim to do. Second, the web-based remailer must not maintain any visitor logs or user information that could potentially fall into unsafe hands and end up identifying you.

You can take anonymity in this method to a further level by chaining remailers - i.e., by sending your email from one anonymous remailer to another, thus driving down the chances of detection even further. You could also combine remailers with an encryption program such as PGP.

Step 2 of 2

Using the remailer service described in step 1, send your email to a **mail2news** gateway. Some are listed below. If you are chaining your remailers, the mail2news gateway will be the final recipient in the chain.

At the time of writing, you can try the mail2news gateways listed below. You need to obtain and read the specific instructions for the mail2news gateway you wish to use for the proper syntax on how to specify the newsgroup to which you wish to post. You can usually receive this information by sending a blank message to the mail2news gateway address with the subject "help".

"To:" Address (mail2news gateways)
- mail2news@reece.net.au
- mail2news@dizum.com
- mail2news@mixmin.net
- mail2news@m2n.mixmin.net
- mail2news@tioat.net
- mail2news@m2n.tophat.at
- or type "mail2news gateway" in your favorite search engine and be prepared to do some digging

If trying to post binaries *and* if the mail2news gateway supports binaries (a big 'if'), you can encode your files and paste the resulting text and binary attachments (if any). Usenet, like email, can only handle text, so encoding is the process whereby binary files (e.g., images or video clips) are translated into text. When you want to post a binary file to Usenet, it may be necessary for you to first translate it into text (i.e., encoding). The most popular encoding and decoding methods are *UU* and *yEnc*. Different utilities are available for each of these methods which are easy to find via your favorite search engine. For more about Encoding and Decoding, see the 'More About' box under the section starting on page 211.

Method 2: Using Your Email Account with a Remailer

It is also possible to post anonymously to a mail2news gateway from your current email account (whether an email client such as Outlook or a webmail service such as Yahoo Mail). You can consult the 'Webmail and Secure Mail Services' section on 203 for some secure email services that you could use for this method.

However, this method is recommended only for more *advanced users* who are sure of what they are doing. Any slip-up can lead to your identifying information inadvertently appearing in the messages.

Please review the detailed discussion in the 'Introduction to Remailers' section starting on page 209. As remailers are changing all the time you should always first check the Usenet newsgroup

alt.privacy for all of the latest information on remailers and always obtain the remailer's latest help file (usually by sending an email to the remailer with the subject "remailer-help").

At the time of writing, here are some addresses you can try:

mixmaster@remailer.privacy.at   remailer@rip.ax.lt

remailer@kroken.dynalias.com   hsub@mixmaster.mixmin.net

remailer@reece.net.au   remailer@dizum.com

or consult the remailer statistics at http://www.noreply.org/echolot/ or http://pinger.mixmin.net/

or type "reliable remailers" in your favorite search engine

1. The **To:** field of your outgoing email / webmail should be addressed to a remailer (not a mail2news gateway) since the message must first be redirected through a remailer

2. The **Subject:** field of your outgoing email / webmail will be irrelevant because the remailer will delete it when stripping the headers from your message, but fill it in anyway if you like (e.g., **Subject: Anonymous Post**)

No matter which remailer you use, the **body** of your message MUST be in the format below. It is *imperative* that your first line begin with 2 colons.

```
::
Anon-Post-To: [insert the newsgroup name]
[blank line]
##
Subject: [this will appear as the Subject of your post]
[any additional header commands - if not, omit this line]
[blank line]
[on this line, start the text of your message or paste the encoded binary file]
```

If the remailer you use does *not* support the **Anon-Post-To:** command, you can instruct the remailer to mail the message to a mail2news gateway as outlined in Method 1. The resulting syntax is shown below (you can use any of the mail2news gateway addresses on the previous page):

```
::
Request-Remailing-To: [insert mail2news gateway address]
[blank line]
##
Subject: [this will appear as the Subject of your post ]
[blank line]
[on this line, start the text of your message or paste the encoded binary file]
```

Your other option when using email or webmail, is to use special mail2news gateway email addresses that are specially tailored for remailers. These special mail2news addresses must be used in conjunction with the **Newsgroups:** remailer command. At the time of writing, you can try the mail2news gateways listed below. As previously stated, you will need to obtain and read the specific instructions for the mail2news gateway you wish to use for the proper syntax on how to specify the newsgroup to which you wish to post. You can usually receive this information by sending a blank message to the mail2news gateway address with the subject "help".

"Request-Remailing-To:" Address (mail2news gateways)

- mail2news@reece.net.au
- mail2news@dizum.com
- mail2news@mixmin.net
- mail2news@m2n.mixmin.net
- mail2news@tioat.net
- mail2news@m2n.tophat.at
- or type "mail2news gateway" in your favorite search engine and be prepared to do some digging

The resulting syntax is shown below:

```
::
Request-Remailing-To: [insert mail2news gateway address]
[blank line]
##
Subject: [this will appear as the Subject of your post]
Newsgroups: [insert the newsgroup name]
[blank line]
[on this line, start the text of your message or paste the encoded binary file]
```

Method 3: Using a Web-based Newsgroup Service to Post Anonymously

As previously mentioned, you can use a web-based Usenet newsgroup provider to access and even post to newsgroups. Some web-based Usenet providers are presented in the 'Web-Based Services' section starting on page 231. However, most of these services require you to register in order to use and pay for the service which may defeat your wish to post anonymously to Usenet.

Here's how you can use the web to post anonymously to Usenet: use your favorite search engine to find websites that have newspost remailer forms, where you enter the name of the newsgroup, the message you wish to send, and the subject of the message. When you click on "send" or "post", the website posts the message on your behalf to the newsgroup you've specified.

One service you could try is **Anonymouse.org's** AnonNews form at http://anonymouse.org/ anonnews.html (see the next screenshot). Anonymouse.org (different from Anonymizer!) has a free, web-based form which allows you to post to Usenet newsgroups anonymously. However, there is no indication as to which newsgroups are supported or the maximum message size.

Figure: AnonForm is Anonymouse.org's newspost remailer form

Over the course of time, newspost remailer forms tend to come and go. You can also try typing "anonymous Usenet post web form" (or similar search terms) in your favorite search engine, and dig away.

This method is probably the easiest of the four outlined in this primer, but the problem with this method is that you may not be truly anonymous as your IP address will be detectable. If the service you use maintains logs of the visitors to their website, you are traceable in theory; perhaps even more so in these days of free web analytics, especially if you are a return visitor.

Some steps you can take to maximize your privacy and anonymity in this situation are:

- Only use services that you trust. To establish trust, search online, read reviews of web-based Usenet providers, and make a decision about who is trustworthy before you start to post

- Use web remailers that support 128 bit SSL encryption

- Use a web proxy or VPN and make sure it is enabled before you post, although please note that not all services may work with a proxy or VPN enabled

Method 4: Using Third-party Software to Post Anonymously

Off-the-shelf software packages are available that do all the hard work of using the proper remailer syntax, encoding the message, and sending the message to a remailer, and then to a mail2news gateway. Some of these programs even encrypt the message so no one can intercept and read it enroute.

Examples of such software programs include **Quicksilver** (http://quicksilvermail.net/), which uses the high security protocol Mixmaster so that your message is multi-encrypted and sent through a chain of remailers. Each remailer strips the information of the previous sender and adds its own to the message before sending it on, ensuring that your message is virtually untraceable.

To see just how complex it can all get, see for example http://users.tpg.com.au/bzyhjr/anon.html (for a software product called **Hamster**).

Jack B. Nymble is a freeware program that uses a series of remailers to make your message anonymous. You can find the latest version of this software on torrent sites. **Private Idaho** is another similar program.

For more information on these and other third-party privacy tools, anonymous remailers and secure web-based systems, consult the postings at **alt.privacy.anon-server** including for the names and locations of anonymous remailers, reliability ratings and software programs that help you stay private and anonymous while posting to Usenet newsgroups.

For even more information, an excellent FAQ on the subject can be found at
http://www.faqs.org/faqs/privacy/anon-server/faq/use/part6/section-2.html.

Chapter 17: Chat, IRC and Instant Messaging

Introduction

Online chatting, including on Internet Relay Chat (IRC), and instant messaging (IM) are ways for people to meet, chat and even trade downloads, all in real time. As with any other Internet activity, you must be careful to protect your privacy and security while chatting and instant messaging.

The Basics of Chat, IRC and IM

If you have heard people talking about Internet chat rooms - they are probably talking about **IRC**. IRC stands for Internet Relay Chat. It is basically a place for people of similar interests to meet in cyberspace and trade conversation (by typing) or downloads (by file transfers).

IRC is the original and oldest type of chatting on the Internet. It remains popular to this day, though by today's standards it represents bare bones chatting and is less flashy, but some people prefer the lack of bells and whistles. All the same chat concepts that you may already know about, such as chat rooms, apply to IRC (chat rooms are called **channels** in IRC).

There are many different software products for IRC, but **mIRC** (www.mirc.com) is far and away the leading IRC software. To use mIRC you have to download the software from their website and install it on your computer. You can evaluate it freely for the first 30 days.

Web-based chatting is also growing more popular as no special software is required; just use your web browser. You can check out web chatting at:

EFnet IRC Web Chat	-	http://chat.efnet.org
XS4ALL Webchat	-	http://webchat.xs4all.nl
TWiT TV IRC	-	http://irc.twit.tv
Mibbit.com Webchat	-	http://www.mibbit.com
freenode IRC Webchat	-	http://webchat.freenode.net

or type "web based chat" (no quotes) in your favorite search engine

Instant messaging or **IM** is chatting but usually just one-on-one with people on your so-called "buddy list" (i.e., people you know or trust; a bit like your email address book or contacts list). IM is like a combination of chat and email in that the communicating is in real time but rather than chatting with the world at large or with people who enter and exit a chat room, your chat session is restricted to only those people you expressly invite (and who accept) or to those that invite you to chat (and you accept).

IM requires its own software, but web-based IM is also growing more popular. For example, IM applications are now integrated in Gmail and Yahoo Mail - all you need is an email account with these websites; when you log in, you can pull up your buddy list within the email window and start chatting with any friend who is online.

What are the Risks?

Chat and IM involve *interacting* with real people in real time (live) as opposed to handling static web pages, mail messages or torrents. As in the physical world, people come in all varieties and with all motivations, so not everyone you chat with may be sweetness and light.

The risks include:

- **People may be faking, masquerading or exaggerating their identity**. The fellow you are chatting with may not be the loving, handsome, fit, single 35-year old that he claims to be. He may be a hateful, ugly, convicted stalker just out on parole. Or he may be a she! The risk of people faking their identities is especially dangerous for kids (see 'Chapter 20: Keeping Your Children Safe' starting on page 281).

- **Abusive language and behavior.** The feeling of anonymity sometimes influences people to say or do things they would never dream of saying or doing in person. Sometimes this is a good thing (e.g., online chatting is great way for shy people to express themselves), but there is a nasty flipside: people sometimes spout hateful, sexist and racist statements.

- **Letting your guard down with personal information**. The casual and carefree environment of chat rooms may lead you to reveal personal information that could be used by identity thieves. The same guidelines you were told about in 'Chapter 5: Social Networking Sites and Online Forums' starting on page 33 also apply to chat and IM: do not reveal your real name, email address, phone number, street address or birthday. You should also never distribute your picture unless to those you supremely trust.

- **Chat and IM reveal your IP address**. As with all Internet activities, your IP address is easily determined. This may allow cyber-stalkers to more easily zero in on you and hackers and snoops to exploit vulnerabilities on your system and launch attacks against you.

- **Running scripts on IRC**. On IRC, scripts are mini-programs that you can run in the background while chatting. Scripts can be quite powerful and make your IRC experience more enjoyable. Scripts can take the form of games or productivity tools. But scripts are also powerful enough to grant a hacker access to the files on your hard drive or allow the hacker to take over your computer. It is easy for a hacker to approach you in a chat room and tempt you to receive and run a script by luring you by saying "This is so cool!"

As a rule, do *not* accept or run scripts unless it is from a supremely trusted source.

- **Direct file transfers**. In IRC, this is called DCC for Direct Client-to-Client. This mode allows you and the user you are DCCing with to establish a *direct* connection and make fast file transfers. You should avoid DCC unless the source is completely trusted because the direct connection exposes you to malware or Trojan attacks from the other user. Make sure your default DCC setting is *disabled* in your IRC software.

How to Stay Safe

- Maintain a healthy skepticism (without becoming paranoid) about strangers that you chat with. Do not reveal your email address or personal information to strangers and be wary about arranging to meet in person. If you do, meet in a busy, public place and let family and friends know about the time and place of the meeting. In particular, do not use your email address or any other personally identifying information as your publicly displayed username or **nickname** (or "nick" for short).

- Block and report abusers. If someone hurls abuse at you online, ignore them, add them to your blocked users list (check your software's help guide), and if warranted report the behavior to the chat room moderator; or, if you were participating in an un-moderated chat, to the system operator.

More About: Moderated Chat Rooms

A moderated chat room is a supervised chat room. A user in the chat room acts as the moderator and keeps an eye on things, provides help and guidance and intervenes when necessary. The extra safeguards afforded by moderated chat rooms are especially good for your kids. Please note that most chat rooms on IRC are *un*-moderated.

- Use a SOCKS proxy to mask your IP address while on chat and IM. This is covered in more detail in the upcoming 'Protecting Your Identity on Chat, IRC and IM Using a SOCKS Proxy' section starting on page 252.

- Consider chatting or instant messaging while logged on to a Windows user account with limited privileges. See 'Chapter 7: Basic Windows Security' starting on page 51 for more details of this technique as it applies to web surfing. This means that, if a hacker does compromise your computer, there is a limit on the amount of damage they can do. Your kids' user accounts should have limited privileges.

- Do not run or install scripts, or open DCC connections unless you know with confidence that the other person you are communicating with can be supremely trusted. Be wary about accepting any files or clicking on any links received from strangers. The same rules for email attachments and links also apply to chat, IRC and IM (see 'Chapter 6: Protecting Yourself from Malware' starting on page 37).

Chat, IRC and IM are Meant to be Fun

Although there are real risks, if you keep up your guard, apply common sense and keep the above tips in mind, you should be fine. Enjoy, and happy chatting and messaging.

More about IRC

Like Usenet and the World Wide Web, you can think of IRC as a distinct element of the Internet. It requires unique software and has its own rules and protocol. As with those other elements of the Internet, there are techniques and software to help you achieve your goals.

What are Channels?

IRC is made up of a list of groups (or **channels** as they are called in IRC) on a variety of topics. The channels are *not* organized in a hierarchy. Instead, IRC is one long alphabetical list of channels at any one time.

Each channel can be thought of as a separate **chat room**. IRC software (often referred to as an IRC "client") will provide you with a list of all the chat rooms that are active at any given time. From this list you can choose a chat room or several chat rooms to enter.

Everyone on IRC is identified by way of a nickname (or 'nick' for short). You can use the same nickname every time you logon to IRC or you can change it as often as you like.

When you enter a chat room, your screen generally will comprise of three parts: participants, the on-going text chatter and a place for you to type your own messages to be broadcast.

Once inside a chat room you will be presented with a list of participants' nicknames. You will also see the messages users are typing in the chat room. IRC also provides for private one-on-one chats (and file transfers) with any person in the chat room (if they accept your invitation to do so). There will also be a portion of the screen for you to type in your own messages. Your messages are not 'sent' to the room for all to see until you press **Enter** on your keyboard.

Some chat rooms are more of a permanent nature while others are set up on an ad hoc basis by IRC users. It is even possible for you to start up your own chat room, but for now, just stick with the existing ones.

You should be able to tell which chat room is discussing your particular interest by its channel name and description. A random screenshot of IRC's channel list is shown below.

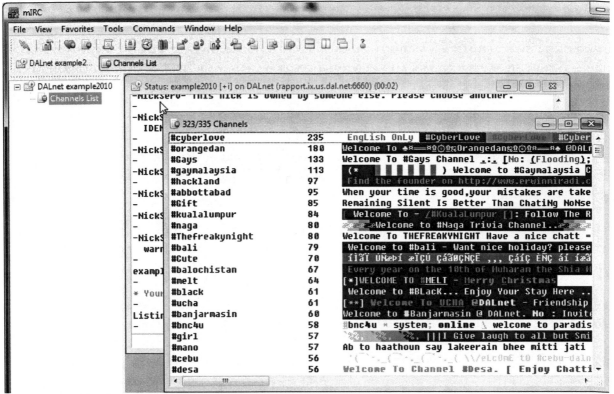

Figure: IRC's channel list can appear a bit of a muddle at first, but a chat room exists for every topic of interest

A Quick Security Note

Although you can choose a nickname and enter alias information in the set-up of your IRC software, you can be traced by your IP address. There are ways to hide your IP address when on IRC (see the upcoming 'Protecting Your Identity on Chat, IRC and IM Using a SOCKS Proxy' section starting on page 252).

! Warning !

Even if obtaining or trading downloads is your goal on IRC, you must be extremely careful as hackers, spammers and snoops are also out there. As with P2P, downloads from IRC are a source of viruses, worms, Trojans, rootkits and other malware.

Fserve

One way of transferring files to and from other IRC users is by using **fserve**. This is a way to invite another user to browse certain folders and files you designate on your computer and let them download the files they want. What is in it for you, you may ask. Well, there is usually a **ratio** imposed on downloading meaning the visitor can only download files after having uploaded some to you.

An fserve session is advertised (usually automatically by way of a script) in the general chat area of a room. The session is initiated by typing a **trigger command** which usually starts with an exclamation point (e.g., "!pics" without quotes). When a person sets up an fserve session they can specify how many people at a time can browse and download files from their computer.

In popular chat rooms, there could be many fserve sessions being advertised with a frenzy of users trying to access them. You have to be patient.

Additionally, most fserve sessions will advertise the specific types of downloads they are seeking. If you ignore their request and upload files of a different variety, you will be kicked off their fserve and possibly **banned** (i.e., never allowed back in). Save yourself the hassle, follow the rules and provide the files they are looking for. It is no good getting banned since a month later when you do have the type of files they are seeking, you will still be banned. If you are banned, this is usually done on the basis of your nickname, but can also be based on your IP address.

Another powerful feature of fserve is that if a user is uploading particularly good files and you want to access their entire collection, you can invite them for a **mutual fserve**. That is, "you let me browse and download from your computer and I'll let you browse and download from mine." This can be done with the ratios in place or on a **leecher** basis - that is, with no upload / download ratios imposed. This is one of the most powerful ways to fill gaps in your collection of downloads; particularly if you come across another collector with the same tastes, but who has different downloads from you.

DCC

Another popular, but less efficient way to trade downloads on IRC is by DCC (**direct client-to-client**). In this method, a private one-on-one chat is set up bypassing the IRC server altogether and the two participants send files back and forth. It is less efficient in that you are not able to browse the filenames of the other person's downloads collection. On the other hand, you can simply ask one another what you are looking for before starting the swapping process.

Fserving is preferred for a number of reasons, including that the handling of user requests is automated. This means that you can concentrate on the files being uploaded to you, assess their quality and ban the jerks that send you crappy downloads.

More About: IRC Downloads

Good guides to downloading on IRC are Ronin's IRC download guide at
http://ronin.soldats.net/leech_guide.html and the IRCHelp download information at
http://www.irchelp.org/irchelp/security/war2.html

Protecting Your Identity on Chat, IRC and IM Using a SOCKS Proxy

Maintaining your anonymity while chatting and messaging is generally more difficult than while surfing the web. IRC and IM users can use a **SOCKS proxy** (sometimes referred to as a WinGate server proxy) to mask their IP address. This is more difficult than using a web proxy for surfing the Internet as the availability of SOCKS proxies is more restricted.

SOCKS proxies act as a buffer for your computer and IP address. This means that the IP address of the SOCKS proxy server will be disclosed rather than your own IP address. For example, any WHOIS or IDENTD commands issued on your nickname on IRC will report the IP address of the proxy server instead of your own. Please note that a SOCKS proxy uses port 1080 while a web (HTTP) proxy uses port 8080.

Top Tip
If you are interested, **ports** are discussed in detail in the 'Ports Explained - An Introduction' section starting on page 59.

Finding a SOCKS Proxy to Use

As with web proxies, you may have some luck typing phrases like "setting up your SOCKS proxy", "configure your IRC proxy", "SOCKS port 1080" (or similar searches) in your favorite search engine.

Also like web proxies and open news servers, some IRC-compatible proxies are listed on websites. Also just like web proxies and open news servers, open IRC-compatible proxies "come and go" due to abuse or due to the operator being made aware of inadvertent public accessibility. Even when they are up and running, their speed may be too slow for your liking. You can make your own decision about accessing IRC with an open SOCKS proxy versus not protecting your identity. You might also opt for a **premium proxy** or VPN service (discussed in more detail shortly).

Some websites listing open SOCKS proxies include:

> **Rosinstrument.com's Free Public Proxy Servers List**
> http://tools.rosinstrument.com/proxy/
>
>> This may not be the easiest site to navigate but some current SOCKS proxy listings are to be found (try the 'quick proxy search' or 'recently checked proxy' options).

Sockslist.net's Always Free Fresh Socks list
http://sockslist.net/

> The list provides a few free listings as an enticement to attract customers willing to pay for access to more comprehensive listings.

Tu-Ilmenau
http://irc.tu-ilmenau.de/all_servers/

> Although not listing proxy servers *per se*, this is a massive list of international IRC servers, including open IRC servers (tick the box "open servers only" to isolate them in the list).

or type "IRC open socks proxy servers" (no quotes) in your favorite search engine.

Using a Foreign IRC server

Using a **foreign IRC server** may be a workable alternative to using an open SOCKS proxy. Connecting to IRC through a foreign IRC server *sometimes* will not reflect your IP address when a WHOIS or an IDENTD command is issued by another IRC user. To try this, simply choose a foreign IRC server when connecting to IRC and, once connected and in a chat room or channel, issue a WHOIS command on yourself to see what IP address is reported.

Setting Up the SOCKS Proxy to Use in Your IRC, Chat or IM Software

Once you are set on a SOCKS proxy server, enter the information in your Chat, IRC and IM software's proxy settings. This is shown in the next screenshot.

Figure: The proxy server settings for the Trillian chat program are under the Preferences menu

---

Top Tip
SOCKS proxies also work with other chat and IM programs, such as ICQ.

Generally speaking, you may be better served by signing up to a comprehensive **VPN service** that supports the SOCKS protocol for Chat, IRC and IM. Some VPN services are presented in the 'VPN Services for Chat, IRC and IM' section starting on page 255.

Of course, any reliance on a third party acting as the middle-man in the process requires a high degree of trust. For example, many services purporting to offer anonymous Chat, IRC and IM state that they are not keeping logs, but who's to say? As tedious as it may sound, you should read the provider's terms of service and privacy policy (usually in the website's 'Legal' or 'Terms of Use' section). Only reliable services should be used and this is not always easy to determine.

VPN Services for Chat, IRC and IM

Below are some VPN services that you can use for chatting and messaging.

Remember that you can often use a VPN service for all of your Internet activities, including web surfing that would otherwise require a separate web (HTTP) proxy. Check the features of any VPN service carefully as you may be able to get more bang for your buck!

Services to Try

SecureTunnel - http://www.securetunnel.com/

> This is a reasonably priced and stable service that creates an encrypted tunnel of your Internet chat, IRC and IM traffic. What is especially likeable is that the technology (a small program residing in your system tray which leaves no discernible tracks behind on your computer) allows you to use and set up proxies for different functions and applications. For example, in addition to SOCKS proxy for *chat/IRC/IM*, you can run an HTTP proxy for your browser and *web ripping* activities (see page 144) and a SOCKS5 proxy for *peer-to-peer* (see page 147). Secure Usenet newsgroup coverage is also offered at a reasonable, bundled price.

Perfect Privacy - http://perfect-privacy.com/

> Perfect Privacy is a VPN service that provides encrypted Internet connectivity and anonymous Internet chat, IRC and IM. Users' traffic is sent through the service's encryption and anonymization servers. Data is decrypted and the user's IP address is stripped and replaced with Perfect Privacy's IP address.
>
> Perfect Privacy's servers cover most of the Americas, Europe and large tracts of East Asia. The service apparently maintains user privacy by not logging information and by providing anonymous payment methods. Its features, which include a large server network, decent server speed and unlimited bandwidth, free switching between servers, unlimited usage, unlimited bandwidth, decent speed, multiple operating system compatibility, mobile devices compatibility and multiple language support, seem to make Perfect Privacy a good value-for-money service.

Steganos Internet Anonym VPN - https://www.steganos.com/us/products/secure-surfing/internet-anonym-vpn/overview/

> Technically, Steganos Internet Anonym VPN is software rather than a service, but with the same result. It provides a secure, encrypted connection to the Internet from its servers in Germany. Steganos Internet Anonym VPN may be suitable for beginners who want an easy solution that provides protection while chatting and messaging.

Testing the VPN

Once you have set up your VPN service, you will need to make sure it is working. The easiest way to test your VPN is at a number of sites on the web. Please see the 'Determining Your IP Address' section on page 141. You can also search for "what is my IP address" (no quotes) in your favorite search engine.

However, while this confirms that your *web browser traffic* (through port 8080) is connecting via the VPN it is no guarantee that your Internet chat, IRC and IM traffic (normally through port 1080) is connecting via the VPN. This is because chat, IRC and IM use a different **port** than web browsers.

A better method is to check using your chat, IRC or IM software itself. For example, after connecting and entering a chat room or channel in IRC, issue a WHOIS or IDENTD command on yourself to see what IP address is reported. It should be the IP address of the VPN service and not your own.

Monitoring Your Ports (Advanced Users)

More advanced users may wish to monitor their active ports to ensure that their Internet chat, IRC and IM traffic is being routed through the SOCKS proxy or VPN service. Ports are discussed in more detail in the 'Ports Explained - An Introduction' section starting on page 59.

A free and recommended port monitoring utility at the time of writing is,

> **CurrPorts** (short for current ports) - http://www.nirsoft.net/utils/cports.html

> > Port monitoring utilities such as this allow you to monitor the connections made from and to your computer. Port monitoring utilities let you see which process has opened which port, shows each connection's local and remote IP address, and may even let you terminate a process. This lets you verify that your chat, IRC or IM programs are properly connecting through your proxy or VPN service.

Process Name	Process ID	Protocol	Local Port	Local Port Name	Local Address	Remote ...	Remote Port Name	Remote Address	Remote Host Name	State
firefox.exe	5144	TCP	62444		127.0.0.1	62445		127.0.0.1	AcerLaptop	Established
firefox.exe	5144	TCP	62445		127.0.0.1	62444		127.0.0.1	AcerLaptop	Established
firefox.exe	5144	TCP	62453		127.0.0.1	62454		127.0.0.1	AcerLaptop	Established
firefox.exe	5144	TCP	62454		127.0.0.1	62453		127.0.0.1	AcerLaptop	Established
iexplore.exe	2748	UDP	58877		127.0.0.1					
iexplore.exe	4692	UDP	62445		127.0.0.1					
RIMAutoUpdate.exe	2752	UDP	54200		127.0.0.1					
Skype.exe	3268	TCP	64080		10.0.0.99	10490		189.69.114.75	189-69-114-75.dsl.tel...	Sent

Figure: A screenshot of CurrPorts a free port monitoring utility

Recommended Software and Tools for Chat, IRC and IM

The applications and tools below are recommended at the time of writing for online chatting and instant messaging (IM).

Internet Chat (IRC)

mIRC (by Khaled Mardam-Bey); $20 after a 30-day trial period - http://www.mirc.com/

> A highly configurable and popular IRC client (Internet chat program). You should also make sure that you always have the latest SERVERS.INI file which is available from the main mIRC site at http://www.mirc.co.uk/servers.html. You need the SERVERS.INI file as it contains an up-to-date listing of all the IRC servers generally available.

Instant Messaging (IM)

Trillian Astra (by Cerulean Studios); freeware - http://www.trillian.im/

> A multi-network chat program that can access your entire buddy lists and, if you like, trade downloads. Incredibly, it supports ICQ, Yahoo!, AIM, Google, Facebook, Twitter, Jabber, Skype, Windows Live, MySpaceIM, and IRC.

IRC Search Engines

SearchIRC - http://searchirc.com/

> A comprehensive and fully searchable collection of IRC networks and channels. The site includes a web-based IRC client. This lets you look for channels of interest and check them out before adding them to your IRC client. The site has a good community section as well.

PART III - SPECIAL INTERESTS

In this part, you will learn how to apply the tips and techniques in this book to your particular interest or hobby.

→ Chapter 18: Are They Up to No Good?

   Do you suspect that your spouse, child or anyone else is up to inappropriate behavior on a computer? Here's how to find out

→ Chapter 19: Workplace and Small Office or Home Office (SOHO)

   How to protect your privacy and security in your workplace, and for your small office or home office

→ Chapter 20: Keeping Your Children Safe Online

   Learn to keep your children safe from online dangers

→ Chapter 21: Shopping Safely Online

   A collection of important tips for staying safe while shopping online and using ecommerce sites

Chapter 18: Are They Up to No Good?

Introduction

Do you suspect that your spouse, child or anyone else is up to inappropriate behavior on a computer? For example, they may be indulging in

- cyber-cheating or cyber-flirting
- pornography
- materials that are hateful, sexist or racist
- materials that violate copyright
- other inappropriate content

There are a number of checks you can do, and most are quick and easy. Detailed steps for these checks are presented below. The steps get more technical as you move along, so stop at your own comfort level or enlist the help of a technically-inclined person if you need some assistance.

If you wish, the steps outlined here can also be used as a way to test and gauge how privately and securely you are going about your own activities.

Checking the Most Recently Used (MRU) Items in Windows

- Look at the computer's **most recently used** files or documents:

    o in Windows, click on the Start button

    o then point your mouse to the selection 'Recent Items' or 'Documents'

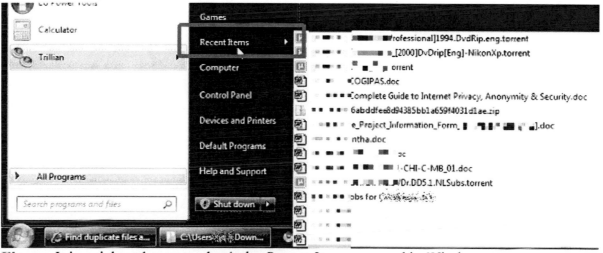

Figure: It is quick and easy to check the *Recent Items* accessed in Windows

- o   you should see a list of the files and documents that were most recently used and opened on the computer

- o   if you then select a document in the list it should open up and you can see for yourself what the file is

    - ▪   if the document does not open or is no longer available, this *may* mean that the file was deleted, moved, renamed, encrypted or originally on a portable hard drive or memory stick.

→ To learn more or safeguard against this, see the 'Clearing Your Most Recently Used (MRU) Records' section starting on page 92.

Checking the Web Browser's History

To look at the Internet browser's **history** of recent websites visited, follow these steps:

- •   open the Internet browser software (e.g., Internet Explorer, Firefox, Chrome)

- •   once the browser opens, look for an icon or menu item called *History*

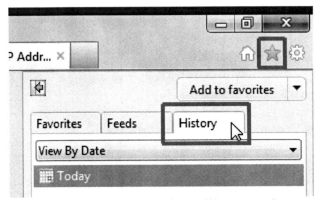

Figure: The screenshot above illustrates how to access the *History* in Internet Explorer 9

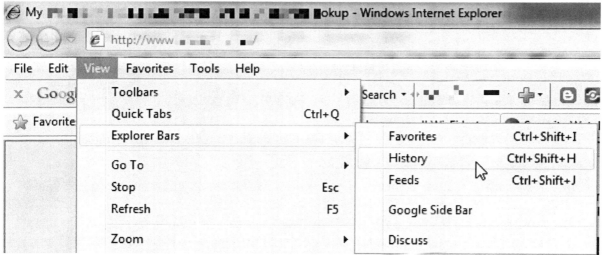

Figure: The screenshot above illustrates how to access the *History* in Internet Explorer 8

Figure: Unless the *History* has been cleared, you should be presented with a list of websites that the user recently visited

> o   scroll through the list of sites to see if all is as it should be. You can also double-click on an item in the list to actually visit the website and investigate further

→ To learn more or safeguard against this, see the 'Removing the Records Your Browser Keeps' starting on page 77.

Checking the Web Browser's 'AutoFill' Feature

Most web browsers now have an **autofill** feature for the search bar. If the feature has not been disabled, the browser retains past search terms. This is meant to be a convenience. When you start to enter letters in the search bar that match past searches, the web browser will display any past matching terms searched or websites visited. This is to help you save time, but can also be a means of detecting past searches.

For example, if you start to enter "cogipas" in the web browser's search bar, it will display any terms searched or websites visited that match the first letters you type in (see the next screenshot).

This is supposed to save you from entering the whole URL, for example, if it is a site that you visit often.

Figure: Chrome's Autofill feature is meant to save you time but reveals past searches and visits

Of course, the same holds true if you enter the term "sex", "porn", "flirt", "movies" or any other word you wish to check. If the term was previously entered into the web browser's search bar or matches a website recently visited, the browser bar will display the full terms searched or URL address of the websites visited (see the next screenshot).

You can experiment with different terms. Ideas for search terms can be found at (uncensored!) lists of the Internet's most frequently used search terms such as http://www.askdavetaylor.com/ what_are_the_most_common_search_terms.html or try typing "most frequently searched terms on the Internet uncensored" in your favorite search engine.

Figure: Unless the browser's records have been cleared, you can determine what searches have been performed or websites visited using the web browser's autofill feature

Or you can even enter a single letter of the alphabet and scroll down the displayed list of matching searched terms or visited websites. This is more time consuming, but more comprehensive.

> → To learn more or safeguard against this, see the 'Removing the Records Your Browser Keeps' section starting on page 77.

Checking the Recycle Bin

Unless the Recycle Bin has been 'emptied', its contents can also sometimes reveal what someone has been up to on their computer.

- On the Windows desktop (the start screen) simply double-click on the Recycle Bin icon to see what files have been deleted recently

- if something looks suspicious, you can right-click on the filename and select 'Restore' to un-delete the file

   o but make sure that you note the 'original location' listed beside the filename since this is the location on the computer to where the file will un-delete (i.e., re-appear). If you do not see the 'original location' details in the list, change your view to Details (shown below). To get to the 'original location' on the computer where the file should now be you can browse to the location by clicking on 'My Computer' and drilling down the described path until you get to the final location

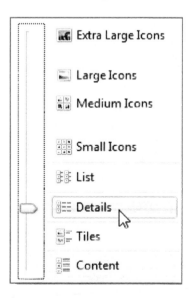

Figure: Undeleting a file from the Recycle Bin

- at the original location you should now see the file and can double-click on it to see what exactly it is (it could be that something harmless has a suspicious sounding filename)

- you could also use a full-fledged file recovery (undelete) utility to see the filenames of deleted data and perhaps even recover in full the deleted files. Many free and easy-to-use file recovery tools exist that can be downloaded and run from a USB stick, thereby leaving no obvious footprint behind on the computer you have scanned. A screenshot is shown below and a detailed example of an undelete utility in action is presented in 'Chapter 14: Wiping Your Sensitive Data' on page 173.

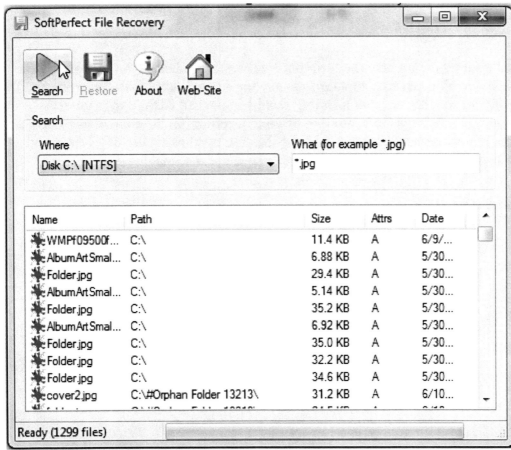

Figure: This screenshot was taken from a popular and easy-to-use file recovery (undelete) utility

→ To learn more or safeguard against this, see 'Chapter 14: Wiping Your Sensitive Data' starting on page 173 and 'Chapter 10: Covering Your Tracks and Washing Up' starting on page 73.

Searching for Terms in Filenames

To search a computer for files that contain inappropriate words or terms in their filenames, follow these steps:

- in Windows, click on the Start button

- type "computer" in the Search box and click on 'Computer' when it is listed (see the next screenshot) or click on the 'My Computer' icon on your desktop

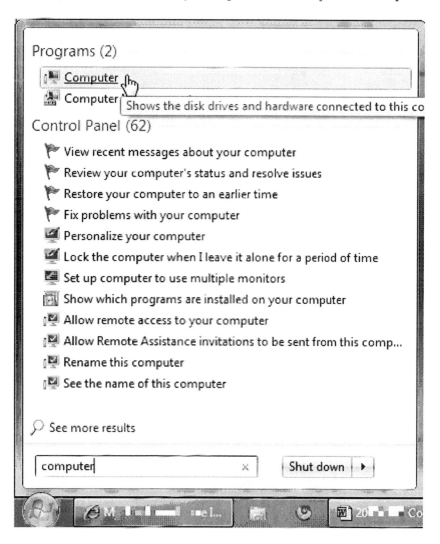

- a 'Computer' window will now open in Explorer. The terms you enter in the upper-right corner of this new window (highlighted below) will be searched on the entire computer

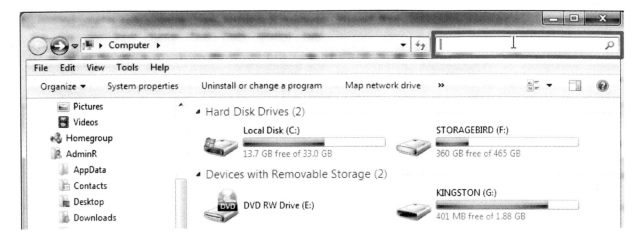

- what search terms you may wish to enter will depend on two main strategies to try. Of course, you can always do two searches that cover both strategies.

    o **Search strategy #1**: by file type or format of file (e.g., images or movies). This strategy may give you lots of wrong 'hits' (files that are OK), but is sometimes best in order to keep the search as wide as possible and, for example, catch files that were carefully named (or renamed) so that they do not stand out.

        - add a search filter by kind (shown in the next screen screenshot); e.g.,
            - Picture
            - Video
            - Document

Figure: Applying a filter by the kind of file; picture files above

- **Search strategy #2**: by subject matter of suspicion (e.g., pornography). This calls for a bit of judgment since you have to think of some keywords that best describe what you are suspicious about.

    o in the search box type in
        - for pornographic material, terms of a sexual nature or 'swear words' including some that you may find offensive
        - ideas for search terms can be found at (uncensored!) lists of the Internet's most frequently used search terms
            - http://www.askdavetaylor.com/what_are_the_most_common_search _terms.html
            - or try typing "most frequently searched terms on the Internet uncensored" in your favorite search engine
        - for copyright materials, use terms like torrent, ripped, rip, DVDrip, Screener

- after a few moments, you will be presented with the results of your search

- simply scroll down the list (it may be very, very long!) and click on files that arouse your suspicion

- and simply continue this process and perform other searches going back to step 1 trying other file types or keywords

→ To safeguard from this, see 'Chapter 13: Encrypting Your Files to Keep them Safe' starting on page 161.

Manually Searching the Registry (Advanced Users)

A bit like searching a computer for files with certain keywords in the filename, this technique searches for keyword in the guts of the computer including program settings, and the names or locations of recently used and opened items.

Accordingly, this technique will often uncover indications of suspicious activities even where the person has renamed, moved, or encrypted files since the programs used to manipulate (e.g., download or open) the files may have recorded the original filename or location of the file.

- Search the computer's Registry for indications that someone is up to no good (whether inappropriate files or chat conversations). The Registry Editor is accessible by typing "regedit" in the Windows start menu (as shown in the next screenshot).

! Warning !

If you have never used the Registry Editor (the *regedit* program) before be careful only to *view* and *not* to delete or change any entries as this could cause a number of serious problems in Windows, including not being able to boot up your computer.

Figure: Starting the Registry Editor

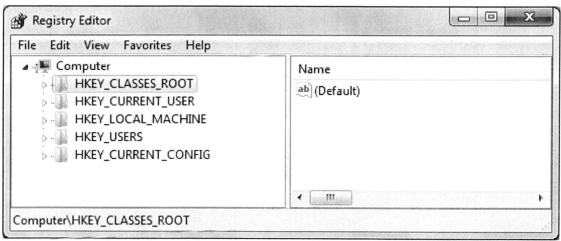

Figure: The look and feel of the Registry Editor is similar to Windows Explorer

- o As you can seriously damage your computer if you delete items in the Registry, make sure you only use the **Edit > Find** command from the menu to view entries, *never delete or do anything else in the Registry for this exercise.*

- o From Registry Editor's menu choose **Edit > Find** (or press **Ctrl + F** on your keyboard). Now type your search term in the dialogue box and click OK. Unlike searching for files, you can only look for one keyword at a time in Registry Editor so do not enter multiple words or you will not get any results.

    - Ideas for search terms can be found at (uncensored!) lists of the Internet's most frequently used search terms
        1. http://www.askdavetaylor.com/what_are_the_most_common_search_terms.html
        2. or try typing "most frequently searched terms on the Internet uncensored" in your favorite search engine

    - For copyright materials, search for terms like torrent, ripped, rip, DVDrip, Screener.

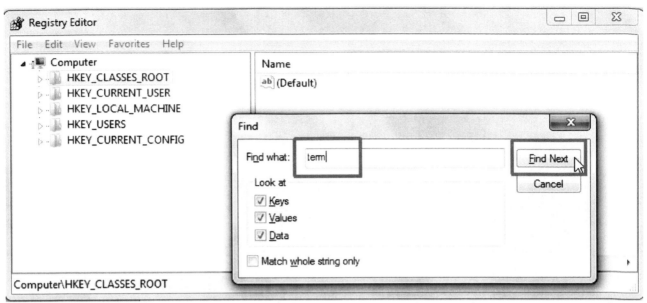

Figure: Using *Edit > Find* from Registry Editor's menu, enter the term that you want to search

Figure: The Registry is large and so the search can take a few minutes

o   You can keep searching through the Registry for this same search term by choosing **Edit > Find Again** from the menu (or pressing **F3** on your keyboard). Keep going until you are told that you have reached the end of the Registry.

   ▪   Make sure hits are actual hits as some words (even swear words) can occur by accident because there are large amounts of raw data in the Registry. Sometimes search hits are not what you first think, so check carefully.

o   When you get hits using this method, you *cannot* then double-click to see, for example, the underlying picture or video file. Rather, seeing such things in the Registry only means that files may once have been downloaded. Usually, you will know 'up to no good' behavior when you see it by a clear pattern that shows up in the Registry.

o   Even if the Registry is clear of what you are suspicious about, this may mean that the user is simply careful because there are software tools to 'clean' the Registry.

→ To learn more or safeguard against this, see the 'Cleaning Your Registry of Trace Data (Advanced Users)' section starting on page 97.

If You Find Some Indications, but No 'Smoking Gun'

Does it look like there may have been some suspicious files, but now they are gone? If you do not find anything or it seems the files were once there but are no longer, this could be because:

- the files could be renamed (e.g., renaming a movie file called SEXY.AVI to look like a boring document called REPORT.DOC)

- the files could be kept on a separate portable device (e.g., hard drives, USB sticks and memory cards that can be plugged into and removed from a computer in seconds and kept in a separate location when not being used)

- the files could be encrypted or otherwise hidden (e.g., the files could be made practically invisible to you unless you know about special software on the computer and, even then, the passphrase needed to decrypt - *un*hide - the data)

- a combination of one or more of the above (e.g., the files could be renamed *and* encrypted *and* kept on a portable hard drive which is kept in a hidden location when unplugged from the computer)

If You are Still Suspicious, but Can't Find Anything

If you strongly suspect inappropriate activity is taking place, but simply cannot find any indications to corroborate your suspicions, you could always (if after checking it is legal to do so!):

- install 'keylogger' software or hardware (see the 'Protecting Yourself from Keyloggers' section on page 29)

- install full-fledged monitoring software (see the 'Consider Using Monitoring Software' section on page 283), especially for your children

- hire a computer forensic specialist that can use special software (see the 'About Forensic Software' section on page 118) which may be appropriate in certain cases

Chapter 19: Workplace and Small Office or Home Office (SOHO) Issues

Introduction

As an employee you must simply assume that you have no reasonable expectation of privacy in the workplace. Also assume that your employer is entitled to record and monitor everything its employees do on the employer's systems, including activities performed at home but using company equipment or Internet access provided by your employer. Businesses can and do record and monitor employees pursuant to the legitimate goals of increasing employee productivity, protection from workplace harassment lawsuits, and preventing the disclosure of confidential information or trade secrets.

Don't Be Stupid

Electronic communications, like email, chat and instant messaging, are especially prone to gaffes and can attract disciplinary measures at work since the informality of these means of communication cause people to be overly candid, casual or careless.

Top Tip
As a rule, do not include anything in a message that you would not want your boss to see.

When it comes to the workplace, it is recommended simply that you follow your company's computer and email policies, period. Even if you delete an email that you regretted sending, it is still likely stored somewhere on the company servers or back-up systems and may, depending on your employer's archiving policies, be retrievable for a long time.

Surfing at Work

Despite the advice above, if for whatever reason you are compelled to pursue personal online activities while at work, here are some ways you may be able to mitigate the risks.

- Use web proxies that not only mask your IP address but which also encrypt and hide the addresses of the websites you are visiting. This way, your employer's logs will display a different site than those you are actually visiting. Good choices are https://www.securetunnel.com/xpress and https://clearlydrunk.com/.

- Delete your browsing history, cache and cookies (see 'Chapter 10: Covering Your Tracks and Washing Up' starting on page 94) as much as possible after a personal web browsing session. However, your ability to do this will depend on your workplace's desktop settings. It is likely that you will have limited privileges and may not be able to do this. If your privileges are limited you will also not be able to download and install washing software, although some utilities can be downloaded and installed to a USB stick at home, and then run from the USB stick at work. A good choice is Free Internet Window Washer http://www.eusing.com/Window_Washer/Window_Washer.htm. But note, even if you can delete your browsing history this is not a great help if your workplace is logging and backing-up all this information separately on its corporate servers.

Physical Security at Work

There is also the matter of physical security for your computer in a workplace setting. Here are some tips:

- When away from your computer, even for only a few moments, lock your workstation. See the 'Using Your Screensaver as Security' section on page 51 for more details but in summary you invoke the lock by holding down the **Windows key** (it may look like a clover leaf on your keyboard) and the **L key** or press the key combination of **Ctrl + Alt + Del** and then select **Lock this computer** from the menu that pops up. It only takes a minute for a rogue colleague, adversary or passerby to snoop your computer and copy or delete files!

- In addition to the screensaver lock described in the tip above, consider *physically* locking your laptop. Most laptops have a **Security Lock Hole** which allows you to secure your laptop much the same way you would your bicycle. Laptops are too easy for thieves to walk away with.

- Be aware of the privacy risks posed by printers and modern photocopiers. Would you believe that a physical printout could be traced back to you? It's true. See 'The Privacy Risks Posed by Printers and Copiers' section below.

- If you are paranoid, you could also periodically check the back of your computer to ensure that no **keylogging** hardware devices (see the 'Protecting Yourself from Keyloggers' section on page 29) have been implanted on your computer by your employer or a rogue colleague.

The Privacy Risks Posed by Printers and Copiers

Would you believe that your print jobs can be traced back to you?

Consider for example: a whistle-blowing employee that sends an 'anonymous' letter to the auditing department in order to expose some wrong doing. Could the exposed senior management use the original letter and somehow track it back to its source, subjecting the whistle-blower to retaliation or worse?

The answer is, yes, it is entirely possible.

How Print-Outs Can Be Traced

Unknown to most people, many major brands of printers leave a unique fingerprint on each printed page they produce. The fingerprint is in the form of too-small-to-see yellow **microdots** that are secretly placed on each printed page. This marker signifies the printer's unique serial number and, in some cases, the print-out's timestamp.

No one seems to know for sure, but there is much speculation that the printer manufacturers implemented this feature under pressure from certain law enforcement agencies.

In a workplace setting it may be therefore relatively easy to trace a print job back to a printer and then, from cross-referencing the printer's activity logs, to the actual person who printed it.

Even in a private capacity at home, your printout with the telltale dots could be traced back to you in combination with the warranty information you may have registered with the manufacturer.

Which Printers are Affected?

To see whether your workplace or home printer uses tracking dots, check the Electronic Frontier Foundation's (EFF) 'List of Printers Which Do or Do Not Display Tracking Dots' at http://www.eff.org/Privacy/printers/list.php.

As there is no practical way of disabling the tracing dots feature, for personal use either steer clear of printers on the EFF's above list or buy a used printer for which you will not register any personal information for warranty purposes. Of course, in the workplace you are stuck with your printer so simply do not print anything personal or sensitive that you wouldn't want traced back to you.

Office Copiers also Carry Risks

Photocopiers represent a different kind of risk entirely. Most modern photocopiers contain a hard drive that temporarily stores copier jobs or collates batch tasks. Unfortunately, like the risks outlined in 'Chapter 14: Wiping Your Sensitive Data' starting on page 173, the data on these copier hard drives are recoverable.

It is no wonder that identity thieves are interested in copier hard drives. If you ever used a copier to copy your financial records, medical information or any other sensitive personal information, it may be sitting recoverable on a copier hard drive somewhere; a treasure trove of information for identity thieves.

Worse, modern copiers, which also act as faxes, scanners and printers, may store those jobs to the copier drive too. Yikes!

How to Protect Yourself

If you own the copier yourself, arrange to have the decommissioned copier's hard drive properly **wiped** or physically destroyed (see 'Chapter 14: Wiping Your Sensitive Data' starting on page 173). As an employee, you can avoid using workplace equipment to copy, fax and scan your personal records. You can also encourage your employer to adopt policies to wipe or physically destroy the drives of decommissioned copiers.

Small Office and Home Office (SOHO) Considerations

Introduction

SOHOs are especially vulnerable as they often rely on broadband Internet access but without the same sort of safeguards that a big company can implement; this lack of scale and funds makes SOHOs a target for hackers. It does not help that SOHOs may keep their Internet connection on 24/7 and have much financial and personal data (e.g., customer and client data) on their computers as part of their operations.

Security and Privacy Strategies for SOHOs

Here are some tips that entrepreneurs and SOHOs can consider to help reduce the risk of security and privacy breaches affecting their business operations.

- **It is paramount that SOHOs set up their wireless network correctly**. You should spend some time reading the instruction manual for your wireless networking hardware equipment, boring as that sounds. It is important to take steps to minimize the threat of someone using your broadband connection without your knowledge. Otherwise, your connection could be taken over, monitored or used to launch attacks on other victims.

  → See the 'Properly Configuring Your Router' section on page 66

- **Use easy, yet powerful encryption technology to lock down your business data** (especially on laptops which are all too often stolen). Encryption software will keep your sensitive information safe, whether from determined hackers or inadvertent disclosure. Think of data encryption as like keeping your files and activities inside an almost impenetrable safe for which only you have the combination. Encryption software is now inexpensive and easy to use.

  → See 'Chapter 13: Encrypting Your Files to Keep them Safe' starting on page 161

- **Make sure to securely wipe, rather than merely delete, data** when disposing of hard drives, USB sticks or even those tiny SD memory cards. Because deleted data and files can be easily recovered using a number of popular utilities, you should know how to properly and permanently delete sensitive data - by *wiping*.

→ See 'Chapter 14: Wiping Your Sensitive Data' starting on page 173

- SOHOs can gain much leverage from using social networking sites, but **be careful what information you share on social networking sites** and do not advertise your absence. Depending on your privacy settings for the social networking site, your posts may be seen by a wider audience than you realize. Inadvertently, you could be advertising a golden opportunity to thieves, corporate spies or adversaries to access your business premises while you are away.

→ See 'Chapter 5: Social Networking Sites and Online Forums' starting on page 33

- Although often overlooked, **use strong passphrases that are hard for hackers to crack**, and use tools to help you generate and remember passphrases. Your online merchant accounts are only as secure as the passphrases you use. Using strong passphrases is a fundamental aspect of your SOHO IT security strategy. Passphrases should be at least 7 characters long and be a mix of at least 3 character types (uppercase, lowercase and numeric). If you have trouble coming up with your own good passphrases there are plenty of tools to help.

→ See 'Chapter 3: Importance of Good Passwords and Passphrases' starting on page 23

- **Keep your operating system up-to-date and use malware scanning and firewall software** to protect against viruses, worms, Trojans, rootkits and other malware infecting your business systems. This can be as simple as making sure that your Automatic Updates feature in Windows in activated (**Start > Control Panel > Windows Update**) and using trusted anti-malware and firewall applications.

→ See 'Chapter 6: Protecting Yourself from Malware' starting on page 33

- If necessary, **keep tabs on any suspect employee computer use** even perhaps with monitoring software. You should always seek legal advice before doing this, just to make sure that you are on safe ground.

→ See the 'Consider Using Monitoring Software' section on page 283

You do not have to go overboard with the extent of your efforts, but some diligence on your part will go a long way to protect the business that you worked so hard to establish and grow.

Chapter 20: Keeping Your Children Safe Online

Introduction

For kids the Internet is a wonderful, expansive place. However, parents know that it is also a place where their children can be harassed, bullied, groomed, stalked, targeted by savvy marketers or where kids might come across inappropriate materials such as sites with themes of a pornographic, racist, violent, gory, hate, disturbing, bizarre or otherwise offensive nature.

Below are some techniques to help keep your kids safe. These child-specific tips are cross-referenced to where you will find the detailed materials in this book.

There is No Substitute for Good Parenting

The same parenting rules that govern in the real world should apply for the online world too. This means trying to get to know what your kids are doing online, participating as appropriate, as well as coaching and mentoring them.

Check-in periodically when your kids are online and ask them about what's going on and, if they chat or instant messaging (IM), with whom. You do not need to do so as an inquisition but rather to show interest. As in the physical world, you want to know what your kids are up to after school on the information super highway.

In a nutshell, spend time with your children online and take an interest.

The SafeKids website's Family Contract for Online Safety is a great way to start the process. There is a pledge that both kids *and* parents can take. This is a good way to get the issues on the table and start the dialogue.

> http://www.safekids.com/family-contract-for-online-safety/

The Basics

As always, the operating system, anti-malware software and firewall should be up-to-date and properly configured on your kids' computer. Part I of this book covers all of these techniques in detail.

If possible, consider having your children's computer (especially for younger kids) in a *common area* such as the family room or living room. This alone can prevent a lot of potential misuse.

The Windows user accounts your kids use should have **limited privileges** (see 'Chapter 7: Basic Windows Security' starting on page 51). This limits both the inadvertent damage they can do on the computer as well as damage that hackers can do should your child's computer be compromised.

In addition, just as you would in the 'real' world, you can introduce a curfew on how long your kids can stay online. Most routers - recall from the 'Properly Configuring Your Router' section starting on page 66 that routers are the small boxes connected to your computer(s) that enable Internet access - can be programmed to automatically stop Internet access between certain times. This can be a very effective way to automatically enforce the curfew; for example, at 9 pm the router simply stops working until 8 am the next morning.

Web Surfing

On the Internet, inappropriate websites are a mere keyword search and click away. It is also possible for kids to stumble on these materials quite innocently and accidentally. For this reason, consider using **site blocking software**. It prevents your kids' computer from connecting to and displaying such content. Though not always foolproof, site blocking software can be a powerful tool in protecting your kids.

The site blocking product that is best for you will greatly depend on your specific needs and the age of your kids. It is recommended that you browse the offerings and read the various reviews to determine what is best suitable for you and your family. You can check:

http://download.cnet.com/ > Windows Software > Security Software > Parental Control

Social Networking Sites and Online Forums

The tips in 'Chapter 5: Social Networking Sites and Online Forums' on page 33 especially apply to kids. Instill in your kids the good sense that they should not disclose their personal information on social networking sites or public forums. They should also never set up meetings in person on the basis of online friendships unless you are part of the meeting and greeting.

Interestingly, it is not just stalkers, hackers, groomers and bullies that you need to be wary of for your kids. More and more, **marketers** are targeting children. This sometimes takes the outwardly innocuous form of games and contests which entice kids to submit personal information. This information is later used to build brand recognition as early as possible or to peddle products and services, sometimes directed at the parents.

Chat and Instant Messaging (IM)

Kids love to chat and instant message (IM), and this may be the hardest sort of Internet activity for you to take an interest. With the right software, you could completely block your kids from chat and IM, but this is probably not feasible or even desirable. You could also use **monitoring software** (see the next section) but that may be somewhat ethically troubling and do you *really* want to know *every* word your kids are typing?

In the end, it may be best to trust your kids but instill in them all the tips for chat and IM found in 'The Basics of Chat, IRC and IM' section starting on page 245, including the 'Top Tips' below.

Top Tip

What your kids must do at the very minimum is,
- don't give out personal information,
- maintain a healthy skepticism that people online may be disguising their true identity,
- don't set up meetings in person without a parent being present, and
- don't accept file transfers or run scripts when online.

Consider Using Monitoring Software

There are a number of monitoring programs available if you want to "double-check" what your kids may be up to online.

Monitoring software records *all* online activity, whether web page visits, email messages, chat exchanges, instant messages, programs launched, peer-to-peer and torrent downloads, and even every single keystroke. The monitoring software can be installed on your kids' computer without them ever knowing about it. Some software will even alert you by email the moment any potentially inappropriate behavior is detected.

> **Spector Pro** (by SpectorSoft), about $100 - http://www.spectorsoft.com/home-solutions.html
>
> This software is not cheap, but is considered the industry leader. It is effective and easy to use.

Chapter 21: Shopping Safely Online

Introduction

Online shopping offers consumers a host of advantages to 'traditional' shopping: there is no need to fight for a parking spot, you can travel from store to store with just a few mouse clicks, and it is easy to compare prices and styles - all from the comfort of your home or office. In addition, shopping online lets you find great deals on the Internet while you browse and socialize at the same time.

However, it is easy to become complacent and neglect the real risks to your online privacy and security posed by online shopping. After all, it is estimated that someone is victimized every seven seconds by online scams.

To help you, follow these easy tips for protecting your online privacy and security while shopping online.

Know Your Merchant

Always spend a few minutes doing some research on the store that you are thinking of buying from. That slick new product for half the BEST price you've seen anywhere else might be too good to be true after all. The web is certainly a 'great retail equalizer'; a place where an entrepreneur can have as good looking and functioning a website as large, bricks and mortar competitors. However, a slick looking website does not always mean that it is legitimate or reputable. If you are buying from an online vendor or an e-store on a larger site such as eBay or Amazon, make sure that the vendor has excellent 'feedback scores' based on many transactions. Looking for seals of approval like **BBBOnline** (http://www.bbb.org/online/) gives you some comfort that there is an actual business behind the website and that it meets a minimum level of proper business conduct.

It is also important to deal with reputable vendors since your purchase data will be on file with them. If the vendors systems or customer databases are compromised by hackers, the hackers may gain further access to your banking or credit card details together with personal data like your name, address and telephone number. Ironically, the information you have been trying so hard to protect from hackers could be disclosed by the sloppy business practices of a third party you entrusted with the same data! Even if the hackers only obtain your username and passphrase, you have already seen the *knock-on risks* this can have (see the 'Different Passphrases for Different Accounts' section at page 24) as this can enable them to infiltrate other sites and services you use.

'S' for Safe

Ensure that the Internet connection is encrypted and starts with https://. An encrypted connection between your computer and the merchant's server helps to ensure that credit card and other details cannot be intercepted. Recall that this protection is achieved through the SSL protocol for web browsers, or Secure Sockets Layer. When it comes time for the online transaction, you should make sure that the address in the web bar starts with https (note the S) and, depending on the browser, that a lock icon appears either in the web bar or the bottom tray.

Figure: Internet Explorer's web bar displays the https and a lock icon, signifying that an SSL connection is established

Careful Using Wireless Networks and Hotspots

Be especially careful when shopping over a wireless connection and simply do not shop using public **hotspots**. If you are shopping over a wireless network (even at home for example) take some simple but essential steps to secure your connection. You must do this to minimize the threat of a hacker or snoop *sniffing* your credit card number or other information literally out of the air without your knowledge. For the same reasons, you should never do any shopping from a hotspot (a public wireless network) since you have no knowledge or control over that network's security settings.

For more information about the risks of wireless Internet see 'Chapter 9: Dangers of Wireless Networks and "Hotspots"' starting on page 63.

Keeping Your System Up-to-date

It is important to keep your system up-to-date including your operating system, malware scanning and firewall software. This can be as simple as making sure that your Automatic Updates feature in Windows is activated (**Start > Settings > Control Panel > Automatic Update**) and using trusted anti-malware and firewall applications. There are some excellent free applications for personal use.

See the recommendations in the 'Recommended Anti-malware Software' section on page 43 and the 'Recommended Firewall Software' section on page 60.

Using Strong Passphrases

Your online accounts are only as secure as the passphrases that you use for them, so do not use poor passphrases. This is one of the most fundamental aspects of your online security. Your passphrases should be at least 7 characters long and be a mix of at least 3 character types (i.e., uppercase, lowercase and numeric).

If you find strong passphrases hard to think up or you are just lazy, get in the habit of using free online tools to help you automatically generate passphrases that are hard for hackers to crack.

See the 'Automatically Generate a Strong Passphrase' and 'Using Tools to Keep Track of Your Passphrases' sections from page 24.

Using Temporary and Disposable Email Addresses

Use temporary or disposable email addresses especially to thwart spammers and identity thieves including when signing up to unknown shopping websites or services. For example, when you initially sign-up you may be sent a confirmation email to which you must reply in order to activate the service. Instead of using your 'real' email address (and it potentially being added to spam lists), use a temporary email address for the confirmation step. Once your account on the website is set up the temporary email address can then safely expire since you no longer need it. This way, you have kept your 'real' email address private and away from potential spammers.

For a list of recommended services, see the 'Temporary and Disposable Email Addresses' section on page 207.

eShopping is Meant to be Fun

Although the risks of online shopping are real, don't be paranoid about them. Have fun and happy eshopping!

COGIPAS 'Top Tips' for Internet Privacy, Anonymity and Security

Needless to say, it is difficult to summarize a book of 300+ pages. However, whether you picked up this book as a novice and read every single page or as an expert and skimmed through it for a comprehensive review, the following concepts should now be well entrenched in your thinking. Even taking the most basic steps will greatly reduce the real risks that the Internet poses to your privacy and security.

You are also encouraged to visit www.cogipas.com for updates and the latest information.

To maximize your privacy, anonymity and security, you should:

1. Construct **strong passphrases** and use free online tools to help you automatically generate passphrases that are difficult for hackers to crack. It is best to change your passphrases twice per year.

2. Keep your operating system up-to-date (whether automatically or manually) and use malware scanning software, including many excellent free applications, to minimize **viruses, worms, Trojans, rootkits, spyware, adware, email/web bugs** and other **malware**.

3. Use **firewall software** (and employ IP address blocking tools) to prevent undesirable sources from connecting to your computer.

4. Use **temporary** and **disposable email addresses** to outwit spammers and identity thieves, especially when signing up to unknown websites or services.

5. Be careful what information you share on **social networking sites** and do not advertise your absence from home or your travel plans or post personal information.

6. Use powerful **encryption technology** to lock down your files and downloads (especially on those all too easy to steal laptops). Excellent software is available, including free software, that will keep your sensitive information safe, whether from determined hackers or inadvertent disclosure.

7. Use a proxy or VPN service to **hide your IP address** from overly curious websites, P2P monitors, identity thieves, hackers and snoops. Use trusted and well-established free **open proxies** or third party 'premium' **proxy** and **VPN services**.

8. Understand that although **peer-to-peer ("P2P")** and **torrents** are all the rage these days, there are serious privacy and security risks in using them. Know what you are getting into *before* installing and using P2P applications. Scan P2P downloads for malware before opening them.

9. **Cover your tracks** and erase the records, including **trace data**, of your sensitive activities that are stored in your web browser, other software and computer. Otherwise, it is all too easy for someone to access these records and breach your privacy.

10. Set up your **wireless network** (whether at home or work) to minimize the threat of hackers stealing or sniffing your bandwidth or sensitive data, hijacking your computer without your knowledge (turning it into a "zombie"), or stealing your identity.

11. Appreciate that deleted data and files on your system can easily be recovered by undesirable snoops; you should **securely remove sensitive data** by wiping it and **purging** empty directory entries. In particular, before disposing of storage media you must **wipe** all of the data on it.

12. Protect your **children** by taking an interest in their online activities and mentoring them in order to help ensure that they are not engaged in **inappropriate behavior** on the Internet.

13. Pause and reflect before clicking on **links** or **attachments** - whether via email, social networking sites, torrent downloads, chat or instant messaging sessions, or Usenet news messages - even when received from trusted sources.

14. Trust your instincts. If something online seems **too good to be true**, it probably is.

15. Be careful and cautious providing **personal information** to *anyone*, but especially to strangers, and always provide only the bare minimum.

16. Be aware that although the risks are real, you do not need to be **paranoid** about them. By implementing the tips summarized here and the techniques described throughout this book you will have taken significant steps to protect yourself.

Glossary

The topics of Internet privacy, anonymity and privacy are not always easy.
To help you, some words and terminology that you may come across are expressed below in alphabetical order in *plain English*.

adware - software that causes pop-up or other advertisements to appear on your computer. Adware is often installed without your express knowledge and is often difficult to uninstall (also see **spyware**)

anonymous remailers - services that allow you to send email messages or post to news groups without any trace of your (the sender's) name or IP address (also see **Cypherpunk remailers**, **mixmaster remailers**, **NYM servers** and **web-based anonymous remailers**)

autotrigger - the name of a mIRC script that automates the trading of files on IRC

AVI - an image compression standard for moving pictures (i.e., a type of movie format)

body - the part of an email message after the headers (the substantive contents of an email message)

bookmarks (see **favorites**)

BIOS - an acronym for Basic Input Output System. The BIOS resides in your hardware and directs how your computer boots up and accesses the operating system

bit (short for binary digit) - the tiniest unit of data, represented by a 0 or 1

brute force attack - a method of defeating security measures by trying all possible dictionary terms, sometimes using supercomputers, to resolve a password or passphrase

byte - eight bits (also see **bit**)

cache - a store of information where your computer can access it rapidly; a **web browser cache** is a database stored on your computer that saves the actual web pages and contents you accessed with your browser. A browser's cache retains information including URLs (web addresses), pictures and other data to make your browsing experience faster. When you request a site, the browser first reloads any data it can from the cache rather than from a distant server on the web. The cache is meant to speed things up for your browser by saving and keeping temporary copies of files you visit (e.g., web pages and images) on your computer

chat (see **IRC**)

checksum - a unique fingerprint for every file; as every data file has an almost unique checksum it is used to verify torrents, images and any other kind of data. For example, forensic software uses checksum methods to verify that an exact copy of a hard drive was made. P2P software uses checksum to verify downloaded torrents. Sometimes checksum is called a **hash** or **hashcheck**

cipher - the form which data takes when converted during the encryption process; for example, when text is transformed into unintelligible data

cluster - the *logical* address space used to describe the minimum amount of *physical* disk sectors to which data may be allocated by the operating system; the smallest space to which data can be saved by your computer's operating system

cookies - small text files downloaded to your computer from a website to help it to identify you. Cookies enable websites to remember your user preferences and settings, track your navigation of the site, offer you extra services or even log on to the site automatically. Depending on your browser settings, cookies may be stored on your computer without your knowledge. Most websites use cookies and some use more than one

cryptography - the science of secret codes; *encryption* is only one form of cryptography

CRC - an acronym for cyclical redundancy check. Your operating system uses CRC values to verify that data has properly been read, copied or moved. If a CRC value differs, your system is able to report back that the data has been corrupted. (also see **checksum**)

ctcp - client-to-client protocol. A particular protocol for offering and getting downloads on IRC

cyclical redundancy check (see **CRC**)

cypherpunk remailers (or "Type I" remailers) - remailers that strip all of the headers from an email message and forward it on to the intended recipient. It is an almost untraceable way of sending anonymous messages, but also means that the recipient will not be able to send you a reply

DALnet - a collection of IRC servers

DCC - an acronym for direct client-to-client. DCC allows you to connect directly with another IRC user, bypassing an IRC server altogether. The 3 basic features of DCC are: Send, Get, and Chat

decoding - a term that describes changing a binary file into a text file so that it can be sent via email or posted to Usenet newsgroups

directory entry - a term for how the Windows operating system records filenames and folder names. **Empty directory entries** are the index entries of old, deleted filenames and folder names

domain name - the name that identifies an Internet website so that you do not have to remember its IP address. Domain names consist of two or more parts, separated by dots; for example, www.cogipas.com and cogipas.com are domain names both pointing to the same IP address for the COGIPAS website

drive imaging - a means of forensically storing everything contained on a hard drive

drive letter - the letter (usually C to Z) that your operating system assigns to one or more logical volumes (drives) on your computer

dynamic IP address - an IP address that is assigned (by your ISP for example) from a block of available addresses each time you connect to the Internet; in other words, you have a potentially different IP address each time you connect

email bugs - invisibly small or transparent images embedded in an email that can be used to track you

encoding - the process of changing a text file received via email or downloaded from Usenet newsgroups into a binary file (e.g., an image or video file)

encryption - the process of converting information into an unreadable form (called a cipher) that cannot be understood unless a decryption key is applied to the cipher; in more layman terms, the scrambling of data to make it readable only by someone in possession of the proper decryption key (usually a password or passphrase)

encrypted virtual drive - a feature of some encryption software that, once enabled, displays encrypted data as another logical drive on your computer; a drive icon pops up on your system much like when you plug-in a USB stick or insert a DVD/CD-ROM

ESMTP - an acronym for Extended SMTP, a type of email protocol

Facebook - a popular social networking site

FAT (or FAT32) - an acronym for file allocation table. FAT is a convention for formatting and keeping track of files stored on a hard drive. FAT32 sets the minimum cluster size at 4k thereby reducing the amount of wasted space or "file slack" compared to the 16k minimum imposed by the older FAT standard (also see **cluster**; **file slack**; **NTFS**)

favorites (or **bookmarks**) - a collection of Internet locations (URLs) stored in your web browser or otherwise on your computer or via an online service that represent websites you want to revisit or that you frequently visit

file extension - normally three letters to the right of a filename's last dot; for example, the file extension of the file `report.doc` is DOC, a file extension for a word processing document

file header - a sequence of data at the start of an electronic file (essentially invisible) used to determined what type of file it is and whether a program can open it. Not to be confused with a **file extension**

file slack - the space between the logical end and physical end of a data file. The **logical size** of a file is the exact size of a file in bytes; this is the size of the file you see reported in Explorer. The **physical size** of a file is the amount of space that the file physically occupies on the disk which is almost always larger than the logical size

firewall - software or hardware that helps protect your computer from external threats by examining incoming connections and data before they reach your computer

forums (aka **message boards**) - areas on websites that allow users to post messages and replies. Forums are a way for websites to build communities

fserve - a way in IRC to access someone else's computer (with their consent) and download from it

FTP client - software used to access an FTP server

FTP server - software that allows other Internet users (clients) to transfer files to and from a server

GIF - an acronym for graphical interchange format, a type of image format with the file extension, *.GIF

Google+ - a popular social networking site

headers - a reference to the collection of the To:, From: and Subject: fields at the start of an email message or newsgroup post; sometimes not all of the headers are visible in your software or reader

history - a record stored in your web browser or otherwise on your computer of the most recent websites you have visited

HTML - an acronym for hypertext mark-up language. Refers to the format used to create and view pages on the Internet's worldwide web

https:// - a reference seen at the beginning of a URL indicating that an encrypted Secure Sockets Layer (SSL) connection is activated for the particular web page

IDENT - a command used to identify a particular user on an (Internet) TCP connection usually using port 13; often associated with IRC and FTP

IM - an acronym for <u>i</u>nstant <u>m</u>essaging, a type of software that allows two or more users to type message to and from one another in real time

IP address - a numerical address assigned to a computer connected to the Internet

IRC - an acronym for <u>I</u>nternet <u>R</u>elay <u>C</u>hat, the original and oldest type of chatting on the Internet. It is basically a place for people of similar interests to meet in cyberspace and trade conversation (by typing) or downloads (by file transfers). Chat rooms are called channels in IRC

ISP - an acronym for <u>I</u>nternet <u>s</u>ervice <u>p</u>rovider, the business from which you get your Internet access from

JPEG - an acronym for <u>J</u>oint <u>P</u>hotographic <u>E</u>xperts <u>G</u>roup referring to a type of image format with the file extension *.JPG

log - a record of a user's download or URL requests on the Internet whether via the Web, P2P, Usenet and IRC; logs are often compiled by IP address

login - the username required to access an online resource and often used in conjunction with a passphrase (e.g., for accessing a website account)

lurker - a term often used to describe a person who (i) enters Internet chat rooms and watches the goings on, but does not actively participate or (ii) browses and downloads Usenet messages but does not upload posts (sometimes also called a "**leecher**")

malware - short for <u>mal</u>icious soft<u>ware</u> which includes viruses, worms, Trojans, rootkits, email/web bugs, spyware and adware

mail2news gateway (or **mail-to-news gateway**) - a process that allows you to post a message to a Usenet newsgroup by sending an *email* message to a specific mail2news gateway address

message boards (see **forums**)

Mixmaster remailers (aka "Type II" remailers) - a type of remailer that adds the security of encryption to Type I remailing technology ensuring that the message is unreadable and untraceable before reaching the remailer (i.e., making it unreadable should it be intercepted or monitored enroute)

MPEG or **MPG** - an image compression standard for video and movie files

MRU - an acronym for '<u>m</u>ost <u>r</u>ecently <u>u</u>sed'

multi-media - a term pertaining to anything audio and/or visual in nature

news server (aka **NNTP server**) - a computer that handles Usenet newsgroup posts and traffic

newsgroups (aka **Usenet**) - the name for a collection of Internet discussion groups

newsreader - software that allows you to read, download and post messages to Usenet newsgroups

ng - shorthand in Usenet-speak for newsgroup

NNTP - an acronym for Network News Transfer Protocol. The protocol used by newsreader software to access Usenet newsgroups

NTFS - an acronym for New Technology File System. NTFS replaced FAT as a newer standard for formatting and keeping track of files on hard drives

nym server - short for anonymous server; a type of pseudo-anonymous remailer

open news server - a news server that is publicly open and accessible at no additional cost

operating system - the software that controls your hardware and all of your other software. Microsoft Windows, Apple O/S and Linux are examples of operating systems

OS (or O/S) - an acronym for operating system

paging file (or **swap file**) - an area on your hard drives used by Windows as virtual memory (i.e., your computer's virtual memory swaps data with its main RAM memory)

pass - short form of **password** or **passphrase**

passphrase - a word or phrase usually needed in conjunction with (i) a login to access an online resource (e.g., a website account) or (ii) software to encrypt and decrypt data

password (or **pass** or **passphrase**) (see **passphrase**)

peer-to-peer (or **P2P**) - a communications protocol for file sharing on the Internet; a way to share downloads on the Internet (see **torrents**)

PEM - an acronym for Privacy Enhanced Mail

PGP - an acronym for Pretty Good Privacy, a suite of privacy software products now owned by Symantec

POP3 mail server - a type of email protocol that allows you to send and receive messages over the Internet. POP3 severs allow you to easily change your settings on the fly as often as you like

private key (or **secret key**) - the decryption key of a key pair (the other key in the pair being the **public key**) used to create digital signatures; your private key (e.g., your passphrase) should not be disclosed to anyone

proxy (or **web proxy**) - a separate computer that acts as an intermediary between your computer and the websites you access with your web browser. Sometimes a proxy server is used to cache popular websites to speed up Internet access, but a proxy can also be used to enhance online privacy as the IP address of the proxy server will be reported to the sites you visit, rather than your own

public key - the encryption key of a key pair (the other key in the pair being the **private key**); your public key may be disclosed to third parties that wish to send you encrypted messages

Registry (or **regedit**) - a collection of files in which Windows stores application and system data. The Registry is accessible with the built-in program Registry Editor

RFC - an acronym for <u>r</u>equest <u>f</u>or <u>c</u>omments; proposed or standardized Internet protocols

rip and **ripping** - the term used for (i) downloading an entire website to your computer including for off-line browsing or (ii) copying songs from a CD, DVD or Blu-Ray (i.e., ripping it); it does *not* mean "rip off"

rootkit - a concealed set of tools on your computer which allow a hacker to continue accessing your system after it has been initially breached; rootkits are often installed at a very base technical level of your system to hide their presence from detection

script - a sequence of instructions executed by an application; a (read) program running on your system

SMTP - an acronym for <u>S</u>imple <u>M</u>ail <u>T</u>ransfer <u>P</u>rotocol, a type of email protocol that allows you to send and receive messages over the Internet (also see **POP3 mail server**)

SOCKS (proxy) - a type of proxy server protocol which derives its name from using *sockets* to keep track of individual connections

spam - unsolicited commercial email

spyware - software that without your express knowledge gathers information about you, including information that may be sensitive like your surfing habits, and which may send this information to a third party. Spyware is often difficult to uninstall (also see **adware**)

SSL - an acronym for Secure Sockets Layer, a protocol that enables encrypted and authenticated communications across the Internet; for example, URLs beginning with "https" for websites represent such SSL connections

static IP address - an IP address that does not change, in contrast to a **dynamic IP address**

steganography (or **stego** for short) - a means of secretly hiding a message or data inside the data of another file, often as text within binary files such as sound or image formats (e.g., *.WAV or *.JPG)

swap file (see **paging file**)

temp - usually short for "temporary" (e.g., the folder C:\WINDOWS\TEMP\ contains temporary data used by the Windows operating system)

TEMPEST - an acronym for Transient Electromagnetic Pulse Emanation Standard, a means of monitoring and reading from a distance what is on your computer screen

torrent - a type of file that facilitates peer-to-peer file sharing on the Internet (see **peer-to-peer**)

tracking dots (or **microdots**) - tiny, usually yellow dots that are secretly placed on printed pages that identify a printer's unique serial number and, in some cases, the printout's timestamp

Trojan - a malicious software program that poses as a legitimate or a useful application; a type of malware

type I remailer (see **Cypherpunk remailers**)

type II remailers (see **Mixmaster remailers**)

URL - an acronym for uniform resource locator, a universal method for accessing locations and documents on the Internet or your local machine with the protocol [HTTP]://[host]/[path]

Usenet (or **newsgroups**) - a completely decentralized collection of many thousands of Internet newsgroups. Essentially a huge database of a mass of newsgroup messages (including attachments) that is continually on the move between the thousands of various computer servers hosting its contents

virtual drive - part of a hard drive used as a storage area for data which, when activated or 'mounted', shows up as a drive letter on your system

web-based anonymous remailers - web-based forms for sending messages through **anonymous remailers**

web bugs - invisibly small or transparent images embedded in a web page that can be used to track you

WHOIS - a service or command that can be used to look up information about who is connected to the Internet; for example, to look up the owner of a domain name or to see the IP address behind an IRC nickname

wipe and **wiping** - the deleting of data by over-writing the physical space on a hard drive where a deleted file previously resided in such a way that the original file cannot be recovered even by forensic software

worm - software that spreads by itself from computer to computer and exploits how the Internet works to cause disruption. Some worms launch distributed denial of service (DDOS) attacks, meaning they attack and flood Internet servers with many requests, blocking or crashing them

WWW - an acronym for world-wide web

zombie – a computer taken over by hackers that may be used to launch unwitting attacks on other computers

Index

THE END

This is the last printed page of this book. If additional blank pages have been added by the printer, rest assured that you have not missed anything. You can use any additional pages for your own notes.

For updates and more resources, please visit,

www.cogipas.com

CPSIA information can be obtained at www.ICGtesting.com
Printed in the USA
BVOW051833310712

296717BV00001B/2/P